The Sabbath Breaker

JESUS OF NAZARETH AND THE GOSPELS' SABBATH CONFLICTS

D. THOMAS LANCASTER

The Sabbath Breaker

JESUS OF NAZARETH AND
THE GOSPELS' SABBATH CONFLICTS

D. THOMAS LANCASTER

Copyright © 2013 D. Thomas Lancaster. All rights reserved.
Publication rights First Fruits of Zion, Inc.
Details: www.ffoz.org/copyright

Publisher grants permission to reference short quotations (less than 400 words) in reviews, magazines, newspapers, web sites, or other publications in accordance with the citation standards at www.ffoz.org/copyright. Requests for permission to reproduce more than 400 words can be made at www.ffoz.org/contact.

First Fruits of Zion is a 501(c)(3) registered nonprofit educational organization.

First Edition 2013
Printed in the United States of America

ISBN: 978-1-892124-68-5

Scriptural quotations are from The Holy Bible, English Standard Version, copyright © 2001 by Crossway Bibles, a division of Good News Publishers. Used by permission. All rights reserved.

Cover design: Anne Mandell

About the Cover: Rembrandt (Rembrandt Harmenszoon van Rijn, 1609–1669) was famous for portraits of his contemporaries, self-portraits, and illustrations of scenes from the Bible for which he often used models from Amsterdam's Jewish population. Our cover is replica of Rembrandt's "The Healing of the Mother-in-Law of Saint Peter," by Tigran Ghulyan (artmaestro.com), based on the Gospel accounts in Matthew 8:14–17, Mark 1:29–34, and Luke 4:38–41.

Cover image ©2013 First Fruits of Zion, all rights reserved.

Quantity discounts are available on bulk purchases of this book for educational, fundraising, or event purposes. Special versions or book excerpts to fit specific needs are available from First Fruits of Zion. For more information, contact www.ffoz.org/contact.

First Fruits of Zion

PO Box 649, Marshfield, Missouri 65706–0649 USA
Phone (417) 468-2741, www.ffoz.org

Comments and questions: www.ffoz.org/contact

Contents

Introduction 1

A Chassidic Tale about Breaking the Sabbath 9

Part One: Sabbath Conflicts in the Synoptic Gospels 11

    In the Grain Fields of Galilee 13

    The Sabbath is Made for Man 25

    Master of the Sabbath 31

    The Sabbath Agraphon 37

    The Man with the Withered Hand 39

    Loosing Bonds on the Sabbath 47

    At Dinner with the Sages 51

Part Two: Sabbath Conflicts in the Gospel of John 57

    The Healing at Bethesda 59

    The Mystical Answer 71

    The Halachic Answer 77

    Healing the Blind Man 83

Part Three: The Thirty-Nine Prohibited Forms of Work 89

    The Thirty-Nine Forms of Work 91

    From Field to Loaf................................. 99

    From Sheep to Fabric............................. 107

    From Hunting to Leather Production and Writing... 113

    Various Acts of Production 117

Conclusion: Judge with Right Judgment 125

    Judge with Right Judgment 127

Endnotes.. 131

Introduction

THIS MAN BREAKS THE SABBATH

Once it happened that the Master and his disciples walked in the holy city of Jerusalem on the Sabbath day when they encountered a man blind from birth. Our Master spat on the ground, made clay of the spittle, and applied the clay to the man's eyes. Then he told the man, "Go, wash in the pool of Siloam." The man went and immersed, and miraculously, he could see.

To heal the man, Jesus spat on the ground and made clay of the spittle. Mixing two substances to form a third is a form of work that Jewish law prohibits on the Sabbath day. Jesus smeared the mud on the man's eyes. Applying a salve or medicine by means of smearing is also considered a form of work prohibited on the Sabbath day. It is a violation of the Sabbath. He sent the man to immerse himself. At least by conventional definition in traditional, Jewish interpretation, immersions are not done on the Sabbath. This single healing incident from the Gospels potentially involves three Sabbath violations.

The Pharisees claimed, "This man is not from God, for he does not keep the Sabbath" (John 9:16). Vocal critics of the Master insisted, "He is a Sabbath breaker."

Do we appreciate the gravity of this allegation?

The Master's enemies wanted to prove that he was a Sabbath breaker because, according to the Torah, breaking the Sabbath is a serious sin for a Jew. God requires the Jewish people to keep the seventh day holy, and cease any labor on it. It is one of the Ten Commandments; it ranks with the prohibitions on idolatry, adultery, and murder. The LORD declared the Sabbath as an eternal sign between himself and the children of Israel—a statute to be observed by Israel throughout all generations. He made it a sign of his covenant with Israel, and he commanded it as an everlasting obligation upon Israel. According to the strictest interpretation of the Torah, a Jew who violated the Sabbath might incur the death penalty:

> Everyone who profanes it shall be put to death. Whoever does any work on it, that soul shall be cut off from among his people. Six days shall work be done, but the seventh day is a Sabbath of solemn rest, holy to the LORD. Whoever does any work on the Sabbath day shall be put to death. Therefore the people of Israel shall keep the Sabbath, observing the Sabbath throughout their generations, as a covenant forever. (Exodus 31:14–16)

Jesus' critics and opponents knew that if they could prove that he was a sinner and condoned sin, they could prove that he was not the Messiah. More than that, if they could prove in a court of law that he himself broke the Sabbath, they had legal grounds for his execution.

BREAKING THE SABBATH

The same allegation is still being lodged against Jesus nearly two thousand years later. "Jesus broke the Sabbath!" But this time it is his followers, not his enemies, who accuse him of Sabbath breaking. Why are Christian interpreters so eager to affirm the Pharisees' allegations against our Master?

From a simple reading of the Gospels, it does seem that Jesus must have been a Sabbath breaker. His disciples plucked grain on the Sabbath; he defended them. He healed people on the Sabbath. He told a man to carry his mat home on the Sabbath. He healed a man with a withered arm on the Sabbath; he healed a man with dropsy right at the Sabbath table of prominent sages; he healed a woman with a bent back, straightening the bent, on the Sabbath.

All of these are obvious violations of the Sabbath. So what's going on here?

Ordinarily these incidents are cited to prove that Jesus was all about abolishing the Sabbath. Traditional Christian interpretation supposes that he did these things to send an implicit message that the Sabbath (along with the rest of the "Old Covenant") is no longer binding. Every Christian Bible reader should understand the absurdity of this proposition. A Messiah who breaks the Sabbath, and advocates breaking the Sabbath is no Messiah at all. He is a false Christ and a deceiver.[1] God himself commands the Jewish people to reject such a Messiah.

THE SABBATARIAN EXPLANATION

Christian Sabbatarians (Sabbath keepers) rightly reject the notion that the Master abrogated the Sabbath. Even Sabbatarians, however, usually interpret the Gospel stories about Jesus and the Sabbath to mean that he did not care about the particulars of Sabbath law. That is to say, he broke the "rabbinic" and "man-made" traditions about Sabbath in order to show everyone that Jewish interpretation of the Law is illegitimate. He let his disciples husk grain on the Sabbath, he healed on the Sabbath, and he made mud and smeared it on a blind man's eyes on the Sabbath all to demonstrate that Judaism had misinterpreted the Sabbath. He did these things to show his followers that the thirty-nine types of labor that Jewish law prohibits on the Sabbath may be safely disregarded.

On this basis, the Sabbath-conflict passages seem to provide believers—even Jewish believers—a license to disregard the particulars of the Sabbath. Christian Sabbatarians make a sharp distinction between the biblical Sabbath and traditional Jewish interpretation of the Sabbath. They teach that Jesus disregarded the latter. Because of this, Jewish believers who choose to be scrupulous about the particulars of traditional Sabbath observance might find themselves accused of legalism by both Gentile Sabbatarians and assimilated Jewish Christians: "Don't you get it? Don't you understand that Jesus overturned the hypocritical legalism of the Pharisees?"

THE MESSIANIC JEWISH EXPLANATION

Neither the traditional Christian explanation (Jesus cancelled the Sabbath) nor the Christian Sabbatarian explanation (Jesus cancelled Judaism) adequately answers the questions raised by the Sabbath-conflict stories. Does a third option exist?

The Messianic Jewish movement maintains that Jesus cancelled neither the Sabbath nor Judaism. Therefore, Messianic Judaism needs to re-examine the Sabbath-conflict stories. This booklet will attempt to demonstrate an internal, halachic (legal) consistency that runs through all of the Gospel Sabbath stories, a halachic consistency that, rather than abrogating the traditional Jewish Sabbath legislation, actually defends traditional observance of the Sabbath. The first part of the book will examine the stories about conflict over the Sabbath in the synoptic Gospels. The second part of the booklet examines the Sabbath stories from the Gospel of John. The third part offers readers a brief introduction to the thirty-nine forms of prohibited labor on the Sabbath.

Most of the contents of this book have been directly excerpted from my work in *Chronicles of the Messiah,* a Messianic Jewish commentary on the Gospels. In addition, an earlier version of this material appeared in print in First Fruits of Zion's *Messiah Journal* issues 104 and 106. The third section regarding the thirty-nine types of labor comes from my work in *Torah Club Volume Five: Depths of the Torah.* This booklet represents an opportunity to assemble all of these pieces in one place for the sake of presenting all the material in a sustained argument.

THE SABBATH AND SUNDAY

This book does not address the question of observing the first day of the week as a Christian Sabbath. Since that practice had not yet emerged at the time of the writing of the Gospel narratives, the question has no relevance to the discussion of the Gospel's stories or Jesus' teaching about the Sabbath. Readers who are curious about the transition from Sabbath to Sunday and the transition from Judaism to Christianity may consult my larger work *Chronicles of the Apostles.* This book is not about arguing which day is the Sabbath. Instead, it confines its interest to the Gospel stories about Jesus and the seventh-day Sabbath.

THE SABBATH AND GENTILES

This book does not deal with the question of a Gentile Christian's obligation to the Sabbath. Since I have confined the discussion to the Gospel narratives, the question about Gentile observance of the Sabbath is not in view. The New Testament narratives do not begin to address the Gentile question until the book of Acts. Readers looking for an argument for Gentile Christian Sabbath observance should see my book *Restoration: Restoring the Torah of God to the Disciples of Jesus.* Nevertheless, a few clarifications on the Gentile question are in order prior to engaging the Gospel material.

The apostles did not require the Gentile believers to keep the Sabbath in the same manner as the Jewish people. They seem to have expected that the Gentile believers would celebrate the weekly Sabbath along with the rest of the believing community (which was Jewish), and they expected that the Gentile believers might even attend synagogue and hear the Torah taught on the Sabbaths, if that is the meaning of James' obscure statement in Acts 15:21. They did not, however, require Gentiles to observe the Sabbath prohibitions on work.

Does this mean that the Sabbath is not for God-fearing Messianic Gentile believers and Christian Sabbatarians? It does not. I myself am a Christian Sabbatarian. I keep the Sabbath as a component of my practice of Messianic Judaism, and I advocate Gentile Christian observance of the Sabbath. The LORD promises to bless and reward even the non-Jew "who keeps the Sabbath and does not profane it" (Isaiah 56:6), but the non-Jew is not obligated to do so. Therefore, when reading the contents of this book, the Gentile believer should not feel any sense of trepidation about being theologically coerced into the Sabbath, nor should he suppose that I am trying to argue him into accepting Orthodox Jewish standards for Sabbath observance. That's not what this book is about.

THE SABBATH AND THE JEWISH PEOPLE

This book does not tell Jewish people either to keep the Sabbath, nor does it argue with Jewish believers who suppose that their obligations to keep the Sabbath have been annulled under the new covenant. At the time of the writing of the Gospels, the idea that Jewish believers were no longer under the Law and therefore no longer beholden to keep the Sabbath had not yet developed in Christian theology. Therefore, trying to muster arguments for that debate from the Gospels will result in an anachronistic misappropriation of the teachings of Yeshua of Nazareth. Instead, this book is only interested in exploring the Sabbath stories and Sabbath teachings in their historical context. That historical context assumes that Jewish people keep the Sabbath as a matter of covenantal fidelity.

As a Gentile pastor and teacher, I am in no position to tell Jewish believers how to keep the Sabbath. While I hope that this book will encourage every Jewish disciple of our Master to reassess his or her relationship to the holy Sabbath, I am not qualified to recommend a halachah (legal code), nor is it my place to tell Jewish people how to be Jewish. That's not what this book is about either. With that said, I hope that the example and the teachings of our Master will inspire his Jewish disciples to enter more fully into the holiness and blessing of the Sabbath day.

THE THIRTY-NINE TYPES OF WORK

To truly understand the issues behind the Gospel's Sabbath stories, one needs to understand the Sabbath legislation from a Jewish perspective. For that purpose I have included a chapter explaining the traditional thirty-nine forms of prohibited activity. I hope that this chapter can dispel some of the common stereotypes and myths about the subject. Every Gospel reader needs to know something about these standards before attempting to interpret our Master's teachings regarding the Sabbath, even if it cannot be historically proven to everyone's satisfaction that all of those standards were in place in the late Second Temple Era. Moreover, both Jewish and Gentile Sabbatarians will find the material instructive and helpful in determining their own individual and community expressions of Sabbath observance.

At the same time, I must emphasize that, in presenting this material, I am not attempting to persuade Gentile Christians to take on a halachic (legal) form of Sabbath observance. Even Judaism itself discourages Gentiles from adopting all the halachic standards of the Sabbath. I believe that Gentile Christians and Messianic Gentiles should celebrate the Sabbath as a day holy to the LORD, but they can accomplish that objective outside of submission to all the legal standards of traditional Jewish law. As far as that goes, since Jewish law prohibits a Gentile from keeping the Sabbath in a manner completely identical to that of a religious Jew, the Gentile who does not adopt all of the traditional prohibitions is actually observing the Sabbath in a more legally correct manner (as defined by Jewish law) than the one who does adopt all the prohibitions.

WHAT IS THIS BOOK ABOUT?

If this book is not an argument for adopting Orthodox Judaism's standards of Sabbath observance, what is this book about? This book is about exonerating an innocent man from false charges. It is about salvaging the Messianic claims of Yeshua of Nazareth and defending him from nearly two thousand years of libelous allegations. This book is about correcting the idea that Jesus cancelled the Sabbath and disregarded Sabbath halachah.

Our Master loved and cherished the Sabbath. He kept the Sabbath as a Jew, and he kept it in the manner of the Jewish people of his day. He attended the synagogue every Sabbath, along with the rest of the Jewish community. He read Torah in the synagogue on the Sabbath, and he participated in the services. He used the Sabbath as an opportunity for teaching about the kingdom, and he used the Sabbath to illustrate the principles of the kingdom. He considered the Sabbath to be a gift to all humanity (not just Jews). He said, "The Sabbath was made for man." He declared that the Sabbath is a day for doing good. He believed that the Sabbath was an appropriate day for the work of redemption because it is his Father's day.

Moreover, this book is about revealing one of the central teachings of Jesus: the priority of love for one's neighbor. As we will see, Jesus loved the Sabbath, but he loved his fellow human beings even more than the Sabbath.

May every disciple of our holy Master who reads and studies this book be blessed with an abundant measure of *Shabbat Shalom*—Sabbath Peace—in the name of Yeshua, who loved the Sabbath.

A Chassidic Tale about Breaking the Sabbath

Yom Kippur is the holiest festival of the year. The Torah calls it a *Shabbat Shabbaton*, the "Sabbath of all Sabbaths," and the Torah strictly warns the Jewish people not to do any work at all on that holy Sabbath of all Sabbaths:

> Whoever does any work on that very day, that person I will destroy from among his people. You shall not do any work. It is a statute forever throughout your generations in all your dwelling places. It shall be to you a Sabbath of solemn rest. (Leviticus 23:30–32)

That explains why the disciples of Reb Schneur Zalman, the founder of Chabad Chasidism, were so shocked to see their holy rebbe break the prohibition against working on Yom Kippur. During the morning prayers they saw him remove his *tallit* and his *kittel* and leave the synagogue. A few of his disciples followed at a distance to see where he was going. They followed him to a small cottage on the outskirts of town where he picked up an axe and chopped some wood. They watched through the window as he used the wood to light a fire in the stove. They blinked in disbelief as they saw him bring water to a boil and prepare a pot of soup. Then they saw him feeding the soup, spoon by spoon, to a bedridden woman, a new mother.

Word had come to the rebbe that the woman had just given birth, but had no one to help her. He knew that her life was in danger, and he prioritized saving her life above keeping the prohibitions of Yom Kippur. When later asked why he did not send one of his disciples as a *shaliach* (an emissary) to perform these tasks, he replied that the opportunity to save a life is a privilege, a mitzvah that he wanted to fulfill with his own hands.

PART ONE

Sabbath Conflicts in the Synoptic Gospels

CHAPTER ONE

In the Grain Fields of Galilee

MATTHEW 12:1–8 • MARK 2:23–28 • LUKE 6:1–5

> At that time Jesus went through the grain fields on the Sabbath. His disciples were hungry, and they began to pluck heads of grain and to eat. (Matthew 12:1)

Jesus and his ever-growing entourage of disciples and followers arrived at their destination along with sunset and the onset of the Sabbath. On the outskirts of a village, the Master and his disciples passed between the wheat fields as the last glow of sunset faded over the Galilean hills. As the first stars appeared, Shabbat officially began, the second Shabbat during the season of the counting of the omer.[2] Passover had come and gone. Spring slipped into summer. Only a few days remained in the month of Nisan. The barley had ripened, and field workers had begun harvesting it, binding it up in sheaves. The wheat took longer. The heads of grain in the wheat fields were still ripening, some still green.

SABBATH BREAKERS

His disciples were hungry, and apparently they had no prospects of a big Friday night meal that night. As they walked, some began to pluck the heads of grain from the stalks of wheat. Luke tells us that the disciples rubbed the heads of grain in their hands to husk them before eating them: "His disciples plucked and ate some heads of grain, rubbing them in their hands" (Luke 6:1).

The Torah seems to allow for snacking from someone's produce as you pass through his fields: "If you go into your neighbor's standing grain, you may pluck the ears with your hand, but you shall not put a sickle to your neighbor's standing grain" (Deuteronomy 23:25), but in the days of the Master, that freedom applied only to hired laborers at work in the field. "Someone just passing through did not have that privilege. It is inconceivable that a wayfarer could pick grain or grapes at will ... In the land of Israel where individual agricultural plots were rather small, such indiscriminate picking would have ruined a farmer."[3] In Jesus' day, picking grain from a grain field while passing through would have been regarded as theft.

If so, why did the disciples feel that they were at liberty to pluck and eat? Given that the barley harvest was already complete or near completion, the disciples had the right to glean. The Torah allowed the poor to enter the fields after the harvesters and glean the standing grain and forgotten sheaves. The Torah also required the harvesters to leave the corners of the field for the poor.[4] The disciples may have been plucking and eating from the still-standing corners of the fields.

Some disciples of the Pharisees were also traveling with the Master. They may have been the same fellows who had sought him out at Peter's house in Capernaum and later complained about him eating with sinners and tax-collectors at the home of Matthew-Levi. They were not antagonists trying to entrap him; they were genuine seekers—associates of the disciples of John the Immerser—who still hoped that Jesus might be an authentic prophet or even the Messiah as John had claimed. Some of those Pharisees might have still hoped that Jesus would yet relent and receive them as his disciples—even if they were old wineskins.

As they passed through the fields that Sabbath, they saw the disciples plucking and husking, and they said to Jesus, "Look, your disciples are doing what is not lawful to do on the Sabbath" (Mathew 12:2); "Look, why are they doing what is not lawful on the Sabbath?" they asked (Mark 2:24). Though Jesus himself did not pluck, husk, or eat the grain, the Pharisees lodged their complaint and posed their question against him. As the rabbi over his school of disciples, he had responsibility for their behavior. By allowing the disciples to perpetrate the alleged Sabbath violation, he endorsed their behavior.

MELACHAH

The disciples' behavior astonished the Pharisees because it violated Jewish interpretation of the Sabbath prohibition on work. Jewish law defines the biblical prohibition on work (*melachah*) as a prohibition on thirty-nine categories of creative and productive acts.[5] The English language contains no equivalent for the word *melachah*. "Work" is a poor translation of the Hebrew term.

The list of prohibited activities includes reaping, threshing, and winnowing. The Pharisees objected that, as the disciples plucked the grain and husked it in their hands, they violated all three.

> Six days shall work [*melachah*] be done, but the seventh day is a Sabbath of solemn rest, holy to the LORD. Whoever does any work [*melachah*] on the Sabbath day shall be put to death. (Exodus 31:15)

The Bible, however, provides a definition for the term. The word first appears in Genesis: "And on the seventh day God finished his work [*melachah*] that he had done, and he rested on the seventh day from all his work [*melachah*] that he had done" (Genesis 2:2). This context defines *melachah* as creative acts of production, including the creation of light, the creation of substance, formation, separation, planting, and creative activities of making, mixing, shaping, and altering—even when those works are performed miraculously or *ex nihilo*. The Torah offers additional definitions by specifying forbidden forms of *melachah* such as lighting a fire, gathering, plowing, harvesting, and carrying, but it never provides what could be considered an exhaustive list of prohibited activities.[6]

The rabbis pointed to Exodus 31 and 35, in which the Torah indicates that the activities required to build the Tabernacle constitute *melachah* and prohibits Israel from performing those acts of *melachah* on Shabbat even for the sake of building the Tabernacle:

> Whoever does any work [*melachah*] on it shall be put to death. (Exodus 35:2)

> Bezalel and Oholiab and every craftsman in whom the LORD has put skill and intelligence to know how to do any work [*melachah*] in the construction of the sanctuary shall work [*melachah*] in accordance with all that the LORD has commanded. (Exodus 36:1)

The sages logically derived the aforementioned thirty-nine categories of work based upon the type of labors required for the building of the Tabernacle. They reasoned that since the forms of creation and craftsmanship required for the construction of the Tabernacle constituted *melachah* prohibited on the Sabbath, they could use those types of labor and activity to arrive at a precise definition of the word. They needed a precise definition for the word because the Torah prescribed a death penalty for the Israelite who performed *melachah* on the Sabbath. Unless the word had tight, legal definition, such cases could only be decided arbitrarily and capriciously.

The accepted list of prohibited activities includes reaping, threshing, and winnowing. The Pharisees objected that, as Jesus' disciples plucked the grain and husked it in their hands, they violated all three.[7] Although the written sources, which document the rabbinic definitions on Sabbath observance, were not recorded until the second and third centuries, the Pharisees' stunned reaction indicates that those definitions, at least in nascent form, already enjoyed popular acceptance in the days of the Master.[8]

> The principal fathers of *melachot* (מלאכות) [i.e., work prohibited on the Sabbath] are forty lacking one: The one who plows, and the one who sows, and the one who reaps, and the one who binds sheaves. and the one who threshes, and the one who winnows, and the one who cleans [by sorting], and the one who grinds, and the one who sifts, and the one who kneads, and the one who bakes.
>
> The one who shears the wool, and the one who bleaches [or washes] it, and the one who combs it, and the one who dyes it, and the one who spins it, and the one who stretches the warp, and the one who makes two loops [across the warp], and the one who weaves two threads, and the one who separates two threads.

> The one who ties, and the one who unties, and the one who sews two stitches, and the one who tears out a portion to sew two stitches.
>
> The one who snares the deer, and the one who slaughters it, and the one who skins it, and the one who salts it, and the one who prepares it, and the one who scrapes it, and the one who cuts it.
>
> The one who writes two letters, and the one who erases a portion to write two letters.
>
> The one who builds, and the one who tears down.
>
> The one who extinguishes, and the one who burns, and the one who hammers with a [hammer], and the one who transports from one domain to another. Indeed, these are the forty principal fathers of *melachot* lacking one. (m.*Shabbat* 7:2)

THE MASTER'S DEFENSE

For most Christian interpreters, the incident and the Master's justification present no difficulties. In traditional Christian interpretation, Jesus allowed his disciples to violate the Sabbath because he had the authority to override the Sabbath. Indeed, he has come to cancel the ritual and ceremonial aspects of the Torah. Therefore, the grain-fields incident is a token of his disregard for the Sabbath and the end of the Torah's jurisdiction. In the new economy of grace, the Law is set aside.

This explanation, however, does not work for Messianic Judaism. From a Messianic Jewish point of view, Jesus neither cancels the Torah nor violates the Sabbath. For him to do so would constitute sin and a disqualification for his Messianic claims. The apostolic community could not have reckoned him as sinless if he violated the Sabbath or endorsed its violation. This tension has led Sabbatarian apologists (along with some Messianic Jewish interpreters) to explain that the disciples were not breaking the written Torah's Sabbath prohibitions but only the "rabbinic fences" and "man-made traditions" around Sabbath keeping. According to this view, Jesus and the disciples held to a literal, *sola scriptura* view of Sabbath observance which does not prohibit reaping by hand, husking by hand, and eating.[9]

If that were the case, one should expect the Master to reply to his critics along these lines: "Hypocrites! Foolish Pharisees who lay your rules and traditions of men upon men's shoulders. Where is it written that picking grain and rubbing it in one's hands violates the Sabbath day? The Torah neither forbids picking grain nor husking it on the Sabbath day!"

In reality, the Torah does forbid harvesting on the Sabbath. Exodus 34:21 specifically prohibits harvesting. What is harvesting? Picking grain. Jesus did not challenge or criticize the Pharisees' interpretation of Sabbath violations.[10] Instead of saying, "No, you are in error. My disciples are not breaking the Sabbath," Jesus admitted that they were breaking the Sabbath, but he defended their right to do so by citing two legal precedents from Scripture: the incident of David with the bread of the presence and the Sabbath-day work of the priesthood in the Temple.

DAVID AND THE PRIESTHOOD

> He said to them, "Have you not read what David did when he was hungry, and those who were with him: how he entered the house of God and ate the bread of the Presence, which it was not lawful for him to eat nor for those who were with him, but only for the priests?" (Matthew 12:3–4)

The Master retold the story of how David, while on the run from King Saul, came to the sanctuary set up at Nob and asked Ahimelech the priest for bread to supply him and his men.[11] Ahimelech replied that he had no ordinary bread, but he did have the twelve loaves of the bread of the Presence. That was the holy bread placed on the table inside the Tabernacle and changed out with fresh loaves every Sabbath. The Torah says that only the priesthood may eat the bread of the presence and only within the sanctuary.[12] Nevertheless, Ahimelech gave David the bread. David took the bread, ate, and left with the rest of it.

The Master briefly retold the story of David and the holy bread as he defended the disciples. He said, "Have you not read what

David did when he was hungry, he and those who were with him: how he entered the house of God and took and ate the bread of the Presence, which is not lawful for any but the priests to eat, and also gave it to those with him?" (Luke 6:3–4).

The story of David and the holy Sabbath bread may have been a common illustration used by the rabbis to discuss Sabbath observance and halachah. The midrashic collection *Yalkut Shimoni* uses the story to prove that the preservation of life takes precedence over the Sabbath:[13]

> It was Shabbat, and David saw that they were baking the Bread of the Presence on Shabbat ... Since he had not found anything there except the Bread of the Presence, David said to him, "Give it to me so that we do not die of hunger, since when there is a case of doubt regarding life, it supersedes Shabbat." How much did David eat on that particular Shabbat? Rabbi Chuna said, "David ate almost seven se'ahs due to his hunger, since ravenous hunger had gripped him." (*Yalkut Shimoni* 2:130 on 1 Samuel 21:5)

Note that the above midrash places the episode on the Sabbath day. The narrative of 1 Samuel 21 also indicates that this story about David may have happened on the Sabbath day—the day the bread was changed out.[14]

The Master admitted that David and his companions did something "which is not lawful" when they took and ate the holy bread. In saying this, he conceded, by way of comparison, that his disciples also did something "which is not lawful" on the Sabbath. David and his men correspond to the disciples. Both parties were hungry and without food. Both parties acquired food by forbidden means. David violated the ritual sanctity of the Temple service by taking and eating the bread of the presence. The disciples violated the sanctity of the Sabbath by plucking, husking, and eating grain on the Sabbath day.

David violated the sanctity of the Temple service because "he was hungry" as were "those who were with him." Jesus justified David on the basis that "he was in need and was hungry, he and those who were with him" (Mark 2:25). Jesus reasoned that the "need" and "hunger" of David and his men provided them with adequate reason for violating the ritual sanctity of the Temple service by eating the bread of the presence.[15]

THE PRIESTHOOD AND THE TEMPLE

> "Have you not read in the [Torah] how on the Sabbath the priests in the temple profane the Sabbath and are guiltless?" (Matthew 12:5)

The Master took the argument a step further, pointing out that the priesthood serving in the Temple must necessarily violate the Sabbath prohibitions. Slaughtering animals, tending the altar pyre, igniting incense, lighting the menorah, baking bread, and so forth all constitute explicit Sabbath violations, but the Torah commands the priests to do so on the Sabbath day.[16] The Master said, "Have you not read in the Law [Torah] how on the Sabbath the priests in the temple profane the Sabbath and are guiltless?" (Matthew 12:5).

Jewish law also points out similar contradictions between the Torah's positive and negative commandments. To reconcile such moral dilemmas, the Talmudic-era sages derived the following axiom:

> Wherever you find a positive commandment and a negative commandment contradicting, if you can fulfill both of them, it is preferable; but if not, let the positive command come and supersede the negative command. (b.*Shabbat* 133a)

The priests violated the Sabbath when serving in the Temple, but they were "innocent" because the Torah commanded them to do so. The positive commandment to conduct the Temple service superseded the negative commandment of the Sabbath prohibitions. In the words of the sages, "The Temple service takes precedence over the Sabbath."[17] How does this argument fit the situation? The priesthood's violation of Sabbath prohibitions for the sake of the Temple service seems to have only tangential relevance to David taking the bread of the presence, and neither example seems relevant to the disciples plucking and husking grain on the Sabbath day. What is the connection between the three episodes? Jesus tied them all together when He said, "I tell you, something greater than the temple is here" (Matthew 12:6).

SOMETHING GREATER THAN THE TEMPLE

> I tell you, something greater than the temple [*Mikdash*] is here. (Matthew 12:6)

On the basis of the two case precedents he cited, Jesus declared the need and hunger of his disciples to be a greater priority than the Sabbath. His argument follows: 1) if the hunger and need of human beings takes precedence over the sanctity of the Temple service (which he demonstrated by David taking the forbidden, holy bread when he was hungry and in need), and 2) if the Temple service takes precedence over the sanctity of the Sabbath prohibitions (which he demonstrated by the priesthood violating the Sabbath to carry out the Temple services), then 3) human need must take precedence over the Sabbath. The logic is simple: The Temple service trumps the Sabbath, and human need trumps the Temple service. "Something greater than the temple is here," namely human need.

If
(Human Need) > (Temple Service)
And
(Temple Service) > (The Sabbath)
Then
(Human Need) > (The Sabbath)

In the Talmud, the sages employ the same pattern of argumentation to defend the use of life-saving medical treatments on the Sabbath: "If the service in the Temple supersedes the Sabbath, how much more should the saving of human life supersede the Sabbath laws!"[18]

Christian interpretations generally prefer to see in Jesus' words that he himself is "something greater than the temple." Accordingly, the reasoning would stutter along as follows: David violated the sanctity of the Temple because he was greater than the Temple service. The Temple service is greater than the Sabbath, and Jesus is greater than all of them. Therefore, his disciples may violate the

Sabbath with impunity because Jesus, who is greater than the Sabbath, allows them to do so.

This conclusion, which amounts to a divine "You're-not-the-boss-of-me" argument, does not arise naturally from the flow of Jesus' argument; nor is it logical. If Jesus was arguing that his Messianic or divine status granted him the authority to set aside the Sabbath at will, then we have returned full circle to the standard Christian interpretation which teaches that Jesus did not keep the Sabbath or require his followers to do so. That same reasoning could be applied to the prohibition on adultery. Jesus is greater than the laws of marriage. Neither does the argument make sense as a halachic (legal) defense. When he said, "Something greater than the temple is here," he could not have been referring to himself. Besides, would the Pharisees have accepted that defense? Instead, the thing "greater than the temple" must be the need and hunger of the disciples.[19]

PRESERVATION OF LIFE

As cited above, a strong parallel to Jesus' argument occurs in the midrashic collection *Yalkut Shimoni*, where David demands his right to the bread of the presence on the basis that he and his men are in danger of starving, and the preservation of life takes precedence over the Sabbath's prohibitions:

> David said to him, "Give it to me so that we do not die of hunger, since when there is a case of doubt regarding life, it supersedes Shabbat." (*Yalkut Shimoni* 2:130 on 1 Samuel 21:5)

That the preservation of life (*pikuach nefesh*, פקוח נפש) takes precedence over the Sabbath is a true and well-attested law in rabbinic literature. Rabbinic halachah (legal procedure) sets aside most of the commandments, even the Sabbath prohibitions, for the sake of saving a human life. The Torah says, "You shall therefore keep my statutes and my rules; if a person does them, he shall live by them" (Leviticus 18:5). The sages interpreted this to mean that a commandment may be set aside to save a life. Life takes precedence over the commandments because it says "you shall live by them," not "die by them." Therefore, the sages derived that it is permissible to violate the Sabbath to save a life:

> A man may profane one Sabbath, so that he may live to keep many Sabbaths. Rav Yehudah said in the name of Shmuel, "If I had been there, I would have proved it [is permissible to break the Sabbath to save a life] with a better passage yet: 'He shall live by them.'" (b.*Yoma* 85b)

In the early second century, after the failed Bar Kochba revolt and in the midst of the horrendous Hadrianic persecutions, the leading, surviving sages of the generation met in Lydda to discuss which commandments a man might justifiably break in order to save his life. During Hadrian's persecutions most outward observances of Torah constituted grounds for arrest, punishment, and possibly execution. The sages decided that, in order to save his life, a man was justified in breaking any commandment except the prohibitions on murder, idolatry, and sexual immorality:

> If a man is commanded, "Break the commandment and you will not suffer death," he may transgress and not suffer death, excepting idolatry, sexual immorality and murder." (b.*Sanhedrin* 74a)

The sages deemed it permissible to break the other commandments in order to save one's life in that the Torah says, "You shall live by the commandments," not "die by them."

CHAPTER TWO

The Sabbath is Made for Man

MARK 2:27

In the previous chapter, we studied the story of Jesus' disciples in the grain fields of Galilee. We saw that the Master conceded that they had broken the Sabbath, but he defended them on the basis that saving life overrides the prohibition against performing *melachah* (work) on the Sabbath. He used two examples from the Scriptures to demonstrate that certain commandments and situations take precedence over the Sabbath prohibitions, making it permissible, and even obligatory, under certain circumstances, to break the Sabbath. The obligation to save life (*pikuach nefesh*), for example, overrides the commandment to keep the Sabbath. When life is in danger, the Sabbath must be set aside to save a life. This line of argumentation, however, raises an important question. Were Jesus' disciples so hungry that their lives were in danger?

MERCY AND NOT SACRIFICE

> And if you had known what this means, "I desire mercy [*chesed*], and not sacrifice," you would not have condemned the guiltless. (Matthew 12:7)

If Jesus' disciples were literally starving to death, and they needed to harvest, husk, and eat the grain or drop dead on the spot, then Pharisaic law teaches that the threat to their lives justified their violation of the Sabbath. But the narrative does not indicate that they were near to starvation—only that they were hungry. The Bible does not tell us how hungry they were, but it is safe to assume that their hunger was sufficient to warrant distress. As surmised above, sunset and the onset of the Sabbath may have overtaken them as they returned from a distant village. They may have walked without food all day, and the Sabbath began as they neared their destination. They may have been faint with hunger. Fasting on the Sabbath is always discouraged.[20] Despite all of this, the passage gives us no grounds to imagine that, if not for the heads of grain in the grain fields, the disciples would have starved to death that Sabbath. Threat to life cannot be reasonably inferred.

Nevertheless, Jesus declared that his disciples were "guiltless." According to his argument, their hunger alone justified the transgression. He rebuked the Pharisees with a quote from Hosea 6:6, saying, "And if you had known what this means, 'I desire mercy, and not sacrifice,' you would not have condemned the guiltless" (Matthew 12:7).[21]

Jesus often used the Hosea 6:6 passage to teach that compassion for human beings, specifically the alleviation of human suffering, takes precedence over ceremonial and ritual concerns. For example, when the same Pharisees criticized him for eating and drinking with sinners and tax collectors, he quoted Hosea 6:6 to justify his choice of table fellowship. He explained that he chose to associate with sinners because, like a physician caring for a sick patient, he sought to alleviate their spiritual sickness:

> But when he heard it, he said, "Those who are well have no need of a physician, but those who are sick. Go and learn what this means, 'I desire mercy, and not sacrifice.' For I came not to call the righteous, but sinners." (Matthew 9:12–13)

The Hebrew word from Hosea 6:6 translated as "mercy" is *chesed* (חסד) which, in Judaism, is generally understood to mean loving-kindness, compassion, and acts of love. In the parable of the Good Samaritan, the Samaritan fulfilled the commandment to love his neighbor as himself by showing the wounded man *chesed* while the priest and the Levite failed to do so on the grounds of ceremonial concerns.

"Which of these three, do you think, proved to be a neighbor to the man who fell among the robbers?" He said, "The one who showed him mercy." And Jesus said to him, "You go, and do likewise." (Luke 10:36–37)

Rabbi Lichtenstein clarifies, "It is not his intention (heaven forbid!) to permit desecration of *Shabbat* (as in the opinion of confused people); rather, the meaning is that [*chesed*] is more important to the Holy One, blessed be he, and so one takes precedence over the other. Likewise, the prophet Hoshea in this verse (Hoshea 6:6) did not intend to nullify the sacrifices, but instead to teach that the internal service of the heart is more important, as he says there, "And the knowledge of God more than burnt offerings."[22]

Mark 12:33 invokes the same passage (Hosea 6:6) when it says that "to love him [God] with all the heart and with all the understanding and with all the strength, and to love one's neighbor as oneself, is much more than all burnt offerings and sacrifices."

> For I desire steadfast love [mercy] and not sacrifice, the knowledge of God rather than burnt offerings. (Hosea 6:6)

Jesus used Hosea 6:6 to teach a principle of placing compassion for human beings and the alleviation of human suffering ahead of ceremonial concerns. In that regard, the alleviation of human suffering is greater than the Temple. Why was it permissible for David and his men to violate the sanctity of the Temple service by taking the bread of the presence? Was King David greater than the Temple? No, he was not, but his human need and desperate circumstance were greater than the Temple service. Jesus applied this ethic to the situation with his disciples. Their need was greater than the Temple service because, like David, they were hungry. Compassion for human suffering is a higher priority than even the Temple service, and since the Temple service is already a higher priority than Shabbat, the disciples were "guiltless" in violating the Sabbath.

THE SABBATH WAS MADE FOR MAN

> And he said to them, "The Sabbath was made for man, not man for the Sabbath." (Mark 2:27)

According to the Master's reasoning, the urgent human need of his disciples took precedence over ceremonial concern for the Sabbath. God desires mercy more than sacrifice. In the Mark version of the story, He punctuated his argument by explaining, "The Sabbath was made for man, not man for the Sabbath" (Mark 2:27). In other words, compassion for human beings should take priority over the Sabbath. The same sentiment was echoed by later, Talmudic-era sages. For example, the Talmud justifies the administering of life-saving medical treatment on the Sabbath by saying, "The Sabbath has been given over to you, but you have not been given over to the Sabbath."[23]

When Jesus said, "The Sabbath was made for man, and not man for the Sabbath," he alluded to the creation narrative where the creation of Adam precedes the sanctification of the Sabbath day, just as the creation of Adam precedes the creation of Eve.[24] God made man before he set apart the seventh day; likewise, he made man before he made Eve. Paul's letters also stress the order of creation: "For Adam was formed first, then Eve" (1 Timothy 2:13). "Man was not made from woman, but woman from man. Neither was man created for woman, but woman for man" (1 Corinthians 11:8–9).

Mark 2:27	1 Corinthians 11:8–9
The Sabbath was made for man, not man for the Sabbath.	Neither was man created for woman, but woman for man.

Perhaps the parallel between Eve and the Sabbath (both of which were created after Adam and for Adam) explains why Jewish tradition speaks of the Sabbath as a queen and depicts the Sabbath as the bride of Israel.[25] It also helps explain what the Master means when he says that the Son of Man is "lord of the Sabbath." The Hebrew equivalent *ba'al HaShabbat* (בעל השבת) might also be translated as "husband of the Sabbath."[26]

THE SABBATH WAS MADE FOR HUMANS

We should make one corollary observation at this point. When Jesus said, "The Sabbath was made for man," his statement includes all human beings, not just Jews. This is not the same as saying that all human beings are obligated to keep the Sabbath in the same manner as the Jewish people. It only means that the Sabbath is God's gift to human beings. It is his blessed and holy day. He did not institute the Sabbath at Mount Sinai; he instituted it immediately after the sixth day of creation, which is to say, immediately after the creation of the first human beings.

A non-Jewish disciple of Jesus does not have the same covenantal obligation to keep the Sabbath that a Jewish person has. Nevertheless, he has the privilege of enjoying the Sabbath, celebrating the Sabbath, and even keeping it to whatever extent he is able. According to our teacher Jesus, the Sabbath was made for everyone.

CHAPTER THREE
Master of the Sabbath

MATTHEW 12:8 • MARK 2:28 • LUKE 6:5

According to all three synoptic versions of the story about the grain field, the Master concluded his exoneration of his disciples by stating, "The Son of Man is lord of the Sabbath."[27] What did he mean?

THE SON OF MAN IS MASTER OF THE SABBATH

One might suppose that he referred to himself. Jesus is certainly lord over the Sabbath and over all things which the Father has set beneath his feet. He often applied the title "Son of Man" to himself. In Hebrew the term "son of man" is (*ben adam*, בן אדם), a common biblical idiom for "a human being." *Ben Adam* corresponds to the Aramaic form (*bar enosh*, בר אנוש), which is also a common way to say "a human being."[28] Ordinarily, the Master used the term—whether in Hebrew or Aramaic we are not certain—in the definite sense: "The Son of Man" as if he was calling himself "the Human Being." He used it as a messianic title, alluding to texts like Psalm 8:5(4), 80:18(17); Daniel 7:13 and passages from the book of Enoch where the divine messiah-figure is called the Son of Man.[29]

In this instance, however, he must have used the term in the general sense of "human being" and not as a messianic title to indicate himself. If Jesus closed his argument with the Pharisees by declaring that he himself is the lord of the Sabbath, it seems to imply that he invoked his divine prerogative to set aside and even break the Sabbath. Again this interpretation fits well with the traditional Christian reading. It argues that Jesus had abolished the Sabbath for his disciples, a power vested in him to do so, because he is lord of the Sabbath.

That interpretation is not satisfactory for Messianic Jewish theology. If we accept that line of reasoning, we must also reject Jesus as a prophet and as Messiah. A prophet who performs signs and wonders and teaches his followers to violate the commandments of Torah is a false prophet. This interpretation falls into the hands of the anti-missionaries and the critics who say, "This man is not from God, for he does not keep the Sabbath" (John 9:16).

In addition, if Jesus meant to declare to the Pharisees that he himself is lord of the Sabbath, then the statement was disconnected from the argument leading up to it. The hunger of David and his men, the work of the priesthood on the Sabbath, the call for mercy and compassion instead of sacrifice, and the notion that Sabbath is made for man and not man for the Sabbath all become irrelevant—swept aside—when he suddenly switched to a new line of argument: "Besides, since I am lord of the Sabbath, my disciples don't need to keep the Sabbath or your silly rules."

THE HUMAN BEING IS LORD OF THE SABBATH

Of course the Messiah is lord of all, including the Sabbath. This too is a sentiment consistent with Jewish theology. Rabbinic literature commonly refers to the anticipated Messianic Era as the ultimate Sabbath of creation. The sages compare the Sabbath to the Messianic Kingdom and refer to it as a foretaste of the World to Come. They compare the waiting for redemption and this present age to the other six days of the week. As king of the Messianic kingdom, the Messiah is lord of the ultimate Sabbath, so to speak. This line of reflection, however, is far afield from the conversation Jesus had with the Pharisees that day in the wheat fields of Galilee. The Pharisees did not know that he was the Messiah, nor was he trying to convince them that he was. Instead, he was attempting to argue, on solid legal grounds, that his disciples were innocent of the charges leveled against them. He was attempting to justify, legally, their picking of grain, not to establish his reputation as Messiah.

Far more likely, Jesus used the term "Son of Man," in this instance, in its more general and common Hebrew sense: a human being.[30] In that case, he concluded his argument by saying to the Pharisees, "A human being is lord of the Sabbath." If so, his conclusion was completely consistent with his preceding argument:

1. Compassion for human need and suffering takes priority over the Temple service.
2. The Temple service takes priority over the Sabbath.
3. Therefore compassion for human need takes priority over the Sabbath.
4. After all, the Sabbath was made for human beings, not human beings for the Sabbath.
5. Human beings are lord of the Sabbath and take priority over it.

By saying that a human being is lord of the Sabbath, Jesus uses a biblical Hebrew idiom to say that human beings are above the Sabbath, not below it on the scale of priority—much as a husband is the head over his wife. In Hebrew, the term "lord" can mean ownership, stewardship, mastery, and as noted above, husband.[31] Just as Adam was the steward over his wife who was created after him and for him, human beings are lord of the Sabbath which was created after them and for them. This reading of the passage seems obvious in Mark's telling of the incident:

> And he said to them, "The Sabbath was made for man, not man for the Sabbath. So the Son of Man [human being] is lord even of the Sabbath." (Mark 2:27–28)

A strong rabbinic parallel to the saying also supports reading "Son of Man" as "human being" in this instance instead of as a messianic title:

> The Sabbath was given to you [i.e., human beings], you were not given to the Sabbath. (*Mekilta* on Exodus 31:14)

In his Hebrew *Commentary on the New Testament*, Rabbi Lichtenstein recognized the argument Jesus was making, and he realized that the logic of the argument demands that Son of Man, in this instance, must be understood in the generic sense as "human being."

> He did not intend to nullify the Sabbath by virtue of the Word of HaShem (the *Logos*) being clothed in him; neither Mattai, Mark, or Luke say anything of the sort, as it appears to me. That interpretation would also present a difficulty in that he himself said earlier, "I did not come to nullify the Torah" (Mattai 5:17). But he himself explains what he means in Mark 2: "And he said to them, 'The *Shabbat* was made on account of man (so that your male or female servant may rest, etc.; Deuteronomy 5:14 in the Ten Commandments), and not man on account of the *Shabbat*. Therefore the son of man is master even of the *Shabbat*.'" The meaning is that man is greater than the *Shabbat*, since *Shabbat* was made on his account.[32]

HALACHAH OF THE MASTER

The incident in the grain fields provides the ethical and legal framework for understanding all of the Master's Sabbath-conflicts with the religious authorities of his day. All of the ensuing conflicts about whether or not it is permissible to heal on the Sabbath center on this one point of contention: Jesus believed that compassion for human beings and the alleviation of human suffering takes priority over ceremonial concern. God desires compassion for human beings above sacrifice and burnt offering.

The Gospels tell numerous stories of Jesus' healing work on the Shabbat, demonstrating that Sabbath-related issues remained completely relevant to the early believers for whom the Gospels were written.

Contrary to popular opinion, the Master does not mean to trivialize the Sabbath or even reduce the rabbinic fences placed around Sabbath observance. On the contrary, he was concerned with restoring a balanced perspective regarding Sabbath observance that prioritizes human need. His conflict with the Pharisees over the particulars of how one ought to observe the Sabbath proves that the Sabbath was an important institution to him, one which he did not lightly dismiss or teach his disciples to disregard. Rather he was concerned that the Sabbath be kept accordingly in the spirit which God gave it.

CHAPTER FOUR
The Sabbath Agraphon

LUKE 6:5

One Greek manuscript of Luke contains an extra verse following the grain field incident. Luke 6:5 in Codex Bezae says, "On the same day he saw a man working on the Sabbath and said to him, "O man, if you know what you are doing, you are blessed; but if you do not know, you are accursed and a transgressor of the Torah."

Scholars agree that this saying does not belong at Luke 6:5. It "is in no sense part of the text of Luke; it is a piece of floating tradition which has come to rest here."[33] A disconnected saying of the Master from outside of the canonical Gospels is called an *agraphon*. Scholars tend to dismiss the authenticity of the Sabbath agraphon.[34] For the sake of argument, though, let's suppose it is an authentic incident from the life of the Master that was passed on orally in the apostolic community until it finally came to rest in the Codex Bezae version of Luke. How might we understand the story and the Master's words?

Traditional Christian interpretation would be quick to use the Master's words as evidence that—for those in the know—the Sabbath was no longer binding. Jesus tells them, "If you know what you are doing—that is, if you are breaking the Sabbath because you know that the New Covenant has cancelled it—then you are blessed; but if you are not aware that I have cancelled the Sabbath and you are breaking it belligerently, then you are accursed and a transgressor of the Torah." This interpretation does not work because it assumes that Jesus cancels the Sabbath and encourages his followers to do so as well. It also assumes two separate standards of righteousness; one for Jewish Christians and the other for Jewish non-Christians.

A better interpretation can be arrived at from the Master's perspective on compassion for human need taking priority over the Sabbath. Jesus believed that human need and the alleviation of human suffering takes precedence over the prohibitions of Sabbath. In that context, he says to the man, "If you know what you are doing—that is, if you are breaking the Sabbath because you have some justifiable reason for doing so, such as alleviating human suffering—then you are blessed; but if you do not know a justifiable reason for violating the Sabbath, and you are simply breaking it belligerently, then you are accursed and a transgressor of the Torah."[35]

CHAPTER FIVE

The Man with the Withered Hand

MATTHEW 12:9–14 • MARK 3:1–6 • LUKE 6:6–11

After telling the story of the incident in the grain fields, all three synoptic Gospels report another Sabbath conflict with religious authorities. "On another Sabbath he entered the synagogue and was teaching" (Luke 6:6). According to his custom, he went to the synagogue on Sabbath morning to join the congregation for the prayers, the Torah reading, and to offer teaching about the kingdom of heaven. "A man was there whose right hand was withered" (Luke 6:6).

A RELATED STORY

The now lost Hebrew Gospel of the Nazarenes had a longer version of the story which explained that the man was a stone mason and that he begged the Master for healing. In his commentary on Matthew, Jerome reports the passage as follows:

> In the Gospel which the Nazarenes and the Ebionites use, which we recently translated from Hebrew to Greek, and which is called by many the authentic text of Matthew, it is written that the man with the withered hand was a mason, praying for help with words of this kind, "I was

a mason, seeking a livelihood with my hands. I beseech you, Jesus, that you restore health to me, lest I must beg shamefully for my food."[36]

The Master's opponents among the sages watched him carefully to see whether or not he would respond to the man's need and heal on the Sabbath day.

HEALING ON THE SABBATH

And they asked him, "Is it lawful to heal on the Sabbath?"—so that they might accuse him. (Matthew 12:10)

Arguments in the Talmud demonstrate that the preparation, application, and ingestion of medicines on the Sabbath day for the purpose of healing remained under debate centuries after the ministry of Jesus.[37] The variety of opinions and legal maneuvers offered in the Talmud suggest that there might not have been complete consensus on the issue of Sabbath healing in the days of the Master. Nevertheless, the Gospels make it clear that Jesus' lenient opinion on the matter was, at best, a minority opinion. In the Gospel narratives, the sages and Pharisees seem to share a unanimous opinion that healing constitutes a violation of the Sabbath.

As students of the Gospels read the Sabbath-healing controversies, they might assume that Jesus argued only with the Jewish interpretation of the Sabbath, not with the Sabbath law itself. In other words, Jesus believed that healing did not constitute *melachah* (prohibited work) and was therefore not a violation of the Sabbath. That is to say, he argued with the sages in order to correct their mistaken ban on healing. He was attempting to reconcile them with a more *sola scriptura* interpretation of Sabbath law which never explicitly prohibits healing.

Tempting as that explanation may be, it has a few critical weaknesses. According to a *sola scriptura* reading of the Torah, the sages over Israel possessed the God-given right to interpret the application of God's laws. Scripture vested them with the legal authority to offer definitive rulings on ambiguities concerning Torah observance.[38] Jesus himself endorsed that authority.[39] For that reason, he did not dismiss the Sabbath halachah to justify healing on the Sabbath; instead, He argued within the halachah for the justification. That is, he argued within the parameters of rabbinic legal discourse.[40]

He never told the Pharisees, "It is permissible to heal on the Sabbath because healing does not constitute a prohibited form of work." Instead, his arguments with the Pharisees all assume that healing is a prohibited form of work. Jesus argued that, even though healing violates the Sabbath, the alleviation of human suffering is a weightier matter than the observance of the Sabbath prohibitions. If he meant to tell them that healing should not be considered a form of *melachah* (prohibited work), then his arguments failed to make logical sense.

One might object that the miraculous types of healing that Jesus performed cannot be construed to be a type of "work" that violates the Sabbath in any sense. On the contrary, miraculous or not, such healings constitute *melachah* by strict definition of rabbinic law in that they result in deliberately changing and transforming something from one state to another state. Just as repairing a leaky faucet on the Sabbath violates the Sabbath, so too repairing a human body breaks the Sabbath.

Another example: Suppose a man had magic powers with which he could light fires. He did not even need a match or cigarette lighter to start the fire, but he could simply ignite a flame by the power of thought. Nevertheless, he would still be in violation of the prohibition on igniting a fire on the Sabbath even if he did so magically. The Torah does not prohibit any particular method of igniting a fire, it simply prohibits igniting a fire on the Sabbath.[41] From this perspective, breaking the Sabbath is not so much about how the work is accomplished, but simply that it is accomplished. If healing is a form of prohibited *melachah*, it does not actually matter how Jesus accomplished it; it still violated the prohibition on work.

TO DO GOOD ON THE SABBATH?

> And the scribes and the Pharisees watched him, to see whether he would heal on the Sabbath, so that they might find a reason to accuse him. But he knew their thoughts, and he said to the man with the withered hand, "Come and stand here." And he rose and stood there. (Luke 6:7–8)

He knew that his opponents were watching him, hoping that he would heal the man with the withered hand so that they would have a basis for denouncing him as a Sabbath breaker and disregarding his teaching. He summoned the man to stand before him. Turning to his opponents, Jesus answered their question by returning it to them. He said, "I ask you, is it lawful on the Sabbath to do good or to do harm, to save life or to destroy it?" (Luke 6:9).

The answer to his first question is "Yes." It is lawful to do good on the Sabbath. To "do good" refers to the performance of a positive commandment. When there is a command to do good, the performance of that commandment supersedes a prohibition which would impede it. As noted in chapter 1, the Talmud says that if a positive commandment and a negative commandment contradict, the positive commandment supersedes the negative commandment.[42] Based upon this principle, Jesus could argue that the positive command of showing *chesed* by alleviating suffering overrides the prohibition against work on the Sabbath.

Is there a positive commandment to heal, though? "Is it permissible to save life or to destroy it?" Jesus asked. According to Jewish law, the Sabbath can be set aside when a medical condition constitutes a threat to life. The Sabbath laws may be breached in any situation in which one's life is at risk, even if the risk is an uncertain one. The Mishnah cites the principle of danger to life overriding the Sabbath as a general rule of thumb. The Talmud makes various arguments to justify the principle:

> Rabbi Mattiyah Ben Charash said, "He who has a sore throat—they administer medicine to him even on the Sabbath because it is uncertain if [the sore throat] might be a danger to life, and any case in which life might be endangered overrides the prohibitions of the Sabbath." (m.*Yoma* 8:6)

> Rabbi Yehudah said in the name of Shmuel, "If I had been in on the argument, I would have proven (that medical attention is permissible) with a better proof-text than the one they used. It is written [in Leviticus 18:5], 'The man who obeys [my laws] will live by them.' It says 'he will live by them'; it doesn't say 'he shall die because of them.'" (b.*Yoma* 85b)

Had Jesus' clients been in any distress which constituted a danger to life, he had license to heal them with impunity. The rabbinic principle of *pikuach nefesh* (saving a life) insures that much. It is lawful on the Sabbath to save life, not to destroy it. The principle of *pikuach nefesh*, however, only applies to life-threatening conditions. The Talmud, for example, forbids the splinting of a broken bone on the Sabbath because a broken bone does not constitute a threat to life.[43]

Neither does a shriveled hand constitute a danger to life. As the official in the synagogue in Luke 13 said, "There are six days in which work ought to be done. Come on those days and be healed, and not on the Sabbath day" (Luke 13:14). Had Jesus been concerned with honoring the prohibition against healing on the Sabbath, he certainly could have waited a few hours until sunset and the Sabbath's conclusion to heal the man's hand.

The Master did not invoke the "threat-to-life" argument as his legal justification for healing. His healings were, strictly speaking, never a matter of *pikuach nefesh*. In his Hebrew commentary on the New Testament, Rabbi Lichtenstein explains, "The opinion of the *Perushim* was that only in the case of saving a life in mortal danger it was permitted to heal, whereas in his words, it is permitted to do good even when there is no mortal danger ... *Pikuach nefesh* (saving a life) takes precedence over *Shabbat*. But in the opinion of Jesus, even when life is not in danger, it is permitted to desecrate it."[44]

On what basis, then, did Jesus justify his decision to heal on the Sabbath?

MERCY ON ANIMALS

> He said to them, "Which one of you who has a sheep, if it falls into a pit on the Sabbath, will not take hold of it and lift it out? Of how much more value is a man than a sheep! So it is lawful to do good on the Sabbath." (Matthew 12:11–12)

No one answered the legal question posed by the rabbi from Nazareth.

As the man with the withered hand stood expectantly in front of him, Jesus posed another question to the sages present in the synagogue: "What man is there among you who has a sheep, and if it falls into a pit on the Sabbath, will he not take hold of it and lift it out?" (Matthew 12:11). One might wonder why this question would even raise a concern, but according to Sabbath law, one may not lift/carry an object (or an animal) outside of an established boundary. Lifting an animal constituted "carrying" on the Sabbath day.[45]

Jesus' hypothetical question might have been a standard rhetorical scenario for discussing Sabbath prohibitions. The Essene community that produced the *Damascus Document* forbade lifting an animal out of a pit on the Sabbath day,[46] but apparently, in first-century Pharisaic-Galilean practice, the priority of rescuing an animal from a pit, even on the Sabbath, was a given. Later arguments in the Talmud take up the same question. For example, in tractate *Beitzah*, Rabbi Eliezer allows a man to lift an animal out of a pit on a Sabbath day only if the animal is required for a festival sacrifice. Otherwise, he prescribes feeding it in the pit to keep it alive.[47] Another passage discusses other options for removing an animal from a pit on the Sabbath, expressing concern for the welfare of the beast:

> Rabbi Yehudah said in Rab's name, "If an animal falls into a pit, one may bring cushions and blankets to put under the animal, and if it climbs out, it climbs out." Another opinion objects, "If an animal falls into a pit, provisions may be made for it in the pit to keep it alive." … Preventing the suffering of animals is a biblical law. The biblical law comes and supersedes the authority of the rabbis. (b.*Shabbat* 128b)

According to the Talmud then, it may be necessary to violate some prohibitions in order to alleviate or prevent the suffering of animals. The Talmud says that showing kindness to animals "is a biblical law," and biblical law, in theory at least, trumps rabbinic mandates. For that reason the sages deemed it permissible to carry provisions to an animal to feed it or to enable it to climb out of a pit on the Sabbath day. All of these fall into the category of "doing good" on the Sabbath, because showing mercy to animals is a positive biblical commandment.

The Master appealed to what must then have been a standard practice, at least in the Galilee: Saving your animal's life took precedence over the Sabbath prohibition on carrying and lifting. At least no one in the synagogue raised any objection to that premise. If that was not an accepted standard of the time and place, Jesus' argument would have lost its rhetorical force. Several men in the synagogue could have simply raised their hands and said, "We would not take hold of it or lift it out."

The Master declared, "Of how much more value is a man than a sheep! So it is lawful to do good on the Sabbath" (Matthew 12:12). The Master argued from the light to the heavy, a method of rabbinic argumentation called *kal vachomer* (קל וחומר).[48] A classic *kal vachomer* argument hinges on presenting a minor case and then stating, "If this is so in the minor case, how much more so is it true in the major case." Thus the logic proceeds from the light matter to the more serious matter: "If it is permissible to violate Shabbat in order to do good to animals and alleviate their suffering, how much more so is it permissible to do the same for human beings?"

GOOD OR EVIL?

So it is lawful to do good on the Sabbath. (Matthew 12:12)

The sages did not answer the Master's rhetorical questions, but if they had, they could have simply said, "It is lawful to save a life on the Sabbath, but if one's life is not in danger, let the matter wait until the Sabbath concludes." Anticipating such an answer, Jesus framed his question in black and white, yes-or-no terms. He literally asked, "I ask you, is it lawful on the Sabbath to do good or to do harm?" (Luke 6:9). He left no room for a "wait until later" answer.

From Jesus' perspective, the question had only two possible answers. One could do good, which was the equivalent of saving life and alleviating suffering, or one could do evil by refusing to alleviate suffering. He categorized the latter option as destroying life. From where did Jesus derive such urgent absolutes? Why must the answer be "yes" or "no," "do good" or "do harm"? He might have been alluding to a prominent passage in the book of Proverbs which condemns withholding good as a sin of omission:

> Do not withhold good from those to whom it is due, when it is in your power to do it. Do not say to your neighbor, "Go, and come again, tomorrow I will give it"—when you have it with you. (Proverbs 3:27–28)

James, the brother of the Master, summarizes the Master's dichotomous, good-versus-evil halachah, saying, "Whoever knows the right thing to do and fails to do it, for him it is sin" (James 4:17).

No one ventured to engage the Rabbi from Nazareth in the halachic argument. The sages and teachers present simply sat in stoic silence, neither affirming his reasoning nor objecting to it. Their silence irritated Jesus. He would have invited further discourse on the subject. "And he looked around at them with anger, grieved at their hardness of heart, and said to the man, 'Stretch out your hand.' He stretched it out, and his hand was restored" (Mark 3:5). "It was restored, healthy like the other" (Matthew 12:13).

CHAPTER SIX

Loosing Bonds on the Sabbath

LUKE 13:10-17

The synoptic Gospels tell another Sabbath-healing story that took place in a synagogue, the story of the woman who could not straighten herself. "As was his custom, he went to the synagogue on the Sabbath" (Luke 4:16). Whenever Jesus visited a synagogue, he packed it out to standing room only. The local synagogue leaders could scarcely object to allowing him the honor of addressing the crowds that flocked in to hear him speak.

WHO STRAIGHTENS THE BENT

On one Sabbath, while he sat teaching in a certain Galilean synagogue, the Master saw a woman bent and crippled by a spirit of infirmity. For eighteen years she had suffered with a condition that might have been *spondylitis ankylopoietica* (a fusion of the spinal bones). She walked stooped over, unable to stand straight.

> And behold, there was a woman who had had a disabling spirit for eighteen years. She was bent over and could not fully straighten herself. When Jesus saw her, he called her over and said to her, "Woman, you are freed from your disability." And he laid his hands on her, and

> immediately she was made straight, and she glorified God. (Luke 13:11–13)

When he saw her, he stopped in the middle of his teaching, perhaps mid sentence. He called her forward. As she shuffled awkwardly through the congregation, Jesus stood to receive her and said, "Woman, you are freed from your disability." He laid his hands on her. She immediately stood straight, completely healed. Luke tells us, she began "glorifying God," a phrase the Gospel writers use to indicate the pronouncement of blessings and praise. The daily morning prayers of Jewish liturgy provide an appropriate blessing for the occasion:[49]

> Blessed are You, LORD our God, King of the Universe, who straightens the bent.

SIX DAYS TO WORK

> But the ruler of the synagogue, indignant because Jesus had healed on the Sabbath, said to the people, "There are six days in which work ought to be done. Come on those days and be healed, and not on the Sabbath day." (Luke 13:14)

By that time, the controversy around Jesus' healing ministry was well-known, and opinions divided over whether or not he should be allowed to continue healing on Sabbaths. "For in the thinking of the Pharisees, it was only permitted to heal on the Sabbath when life was in danger, and here there is no mortal danger, and they could wait until after the Sabbath."[50]

The dramatic and public healing that day placed the synagogue official in an awkward position. If he simply ignored the matter, that might appear as a tacit endorsement and incite the ire of several of his conservative congregants. On the other hand, if he condemned the healing outright, he would incite the disapproval of the crowds and the many disciples of Jesus present that day. He did not venture to offer the Master a direct rebuke. Instead, he tactfully turned the rebuke toward the people in attendance, saying,

"There are six days in which work should be done; so come during them and get healed, and not on the Sabbath day."

If the Master believed that healing did not constitute a violation of the Sabbath, he would have said so at that point. Instead, his ensuing argument assumed that healing does violate the Sabbath, but he argued that *chesed* (mercy) for a human being should take precedence over Sabbath prohibitions:

> Then the LORD answered him, "You hypocrites! Does not each of you on the Sabbath untie his ox or his donkey from the manger and lead it away to water it? And ought not this woman, a daughter of Abraham whom Satan bound for eighteen years, be loosed from this bond on the Sabbath day?" (Luke 13:15–16)

Jewish Sabbath-laws prohibit the tying and untying of certain types of knots on the Sabbath day. Both tying and untying can constitute *melachah*, prohibited forms of work on the Sabbath day. The sages, however, specifically permitted the tying and untying of knots for the purpose of leashing animals and drawing water.[51] The Talmud also teaches that one can lead a horse to water, but he cannot make him drink:

> Is it not taught that a man must not fill a bucket with water and hold it in front of his beast on the Sabbath? Instead he fills his bucket and pours it into a trough and the cow drinks on his own accord (b.*Eruvin* 20b)

Jesus took it for granted that tying and untying knots violates the Sabbath.[52] He also took it for granted that an exception must be made for the sake of watering one's animal. In this case, the owner of the animal violates the Sabbath prohibitions merely for the sake of alleviating the animal's discomfort—so that it does not suffer from thirst. Immediate threat to life is not necessarily in view. Surely the animal's thirst could be slated after the Sabbath's conclusion.

Having established that the accepted *halachah* (legal interpretation) permitted violating some Sabbath prohibitions in order to prevent suffering to animals, Jesus reasoned from the light to the heavy (*kal vachomer*, קל וחומר): How much more so then is it permissible to violate the Sabbath in order to alleviate the suffering of a human being?

Most Gospel readers probably would not consider the mere tying or untying of a knot to constitute *melachah,* a form of work forbidden on the Sabbath, but apparently Jesus did. If he considered tying or untying as actually permissible on Sabbath, his argument loses all its force.

Our Master established that quenching the thirst of an animal justified temporarily violating the Sabbath by loosing the knot with which it was bound. If so, surely a daughter of Abraham, whom Satan bound for eighteen years, should be "loosed" from her bond on the Sabbath day rather than having to wait until the conclusion of the Sabbath. By loosing Satan's captive the Master fulfilled the prophecy that says, "He has sent me to proclaim liberty to the captives" (Luke 4:18).

Jesus' critics did not have any answer, but the common people rejoiced in the miracle.

CHAPTER SEVEN
At Dinner with the Sages

LUKE 14:1–6

Our Master Jesus loved the Sabbath. His teaching and healing ministry seemed to revolve around the Sabbath day. The Sabbath typically found him as the guest speaker in a synagogue teaching about the kingdom, or as a dinner guest in someone's home. The Sabbath observant family honored the Sabbath with three festive meals: The first meal welcomed the Sabbath on Friday night, the second meal came after the Sabbath morning synagogue service, and the third meal bade the Sabbath farewell shortly before sunset.

Once, it happened that one of the prominent Pharisees invited our Master in for one of the meals of the Sabbath.[53] The prominent Pharisee had disciples of his own. If Luke had provided the man's full name, we might be able to identify him as one of the sages of the late Second Temple period.

> One Sabbath, when he went to dine at the house of a ruler of the Pharisees, they were watching him carefully. (Luke 14:1)

The Pharisees harbored contradictory opinions regarding Jesus. Some reviled him and sought his demise, but many found him intriguing. They followed him, studied him, criticized him, and very often, invited him home for a Sabbath meal.

The fact that the Pharisees continually brought Jesus into their meals and fellowship indicates that they considered him one of their own.

DINNER WITH THE SAGES

A Sabbath meal in the home of a Torah sage was a splendid affair. The rabbis placed before their guests the best that the marketplace had to offer. They served the best meats, breads, and wines they could afford in honor of the Sabbath. The disciples of the sage became guests in his home where they crowded about their teacher's table to enjoy the Sabbath peace together. The conversation always turned to the matters of Torah:

> Rabbi Shimon (ben Yochai) said, "If three have eaten at one table and have not exchanged at it some words of Torah, it is as if they had eaten sacrifices to the dead ... But, if three have eaten at one table and have exchanged some words of Torah, it is as if they had eaten at the table of the Almighty, blessed be He, as it is said [in Ezekiel 41:22], 'This is the table before the LORD.'" (m.*Avot* 3.3)

In this case, the prominent Pharisee invited Jesus to his table specifically regarding a certain matter of Torah. Perhaps the disciples of that particular sage had engaged in the argument over whether or not healing justifies violating the Sabbath. The argument may well have ensued after hearing reports of the controversy around Jesus of Nazareth. The theological conundrum created by Jesus' seemingly divine, Sabbath-day healings must have piqued their acute interest in the question. If such healings did indeed constitute a violation of the Sabbath, why did God validate them through this man? One can imagine the argument that initiated the dinner invitation. "How can he be a real prophet if he heals on the Sabbath?" "But is it really a sin to heal on the Sabbath?" "Let's invite the man and see what he will say," they might have suggested.

A HEALING AT THE TABLE

> "And Jesus responded to the lawyers and Pharisees, saying, 'Is it lawful to heal on the Sabbath, or not?'" (Luke 14:3)

When our Master Jesus came to recline in their midst, they seated him across from a man who suffered from dropsy, perhaps some swelling like edema. Would the healer perform one of his controversial healings? "They were watching him carefully" (Luke 14:1).

Jesus took the bait, but first he deferred the matter to his host. The Pharisees considered offering a legal decision in the presence of one's teacher or an esteemed rabbi without his consent a serious social taboo and an act of impertinence.[54] Even if the teacher was not one's own teacher, the sages refrained from offering a legal opinion in the presence of an older teacher. Those who ignored the convention received chastisement. Jesus decorously navigated the situation by offering his host the opportunity to render a legal opinion first. He asked them, "Is it lawful to heal on the Sabbath or not?" (Luke 14:3). Only after his host and his host's disciples all declined to comment did Jesus offer his opinion.

Torah sages and rabbis were accustomed to routinely answering legal questions pertaining to the Sabbath. The Master's question was not as straightforward as it sounds. He was not asking for advice; he invited them to engage him in the argument. None of them ventured to offer an answer or spar with the Master. They themselves felt a measure of uncertainty about the question. Jesus took their reticence as tacit approval. He healed the man, and then offered his halachic justification for doing so.

One might consider the miraculous hand of God as justification enough. Why argue further? If God frowned upon healing on the Sabbath, why would he have endorsed it by enabling Jesus to accomplish it? Such simple reasoning, however, would not satisfy the minds of men trained in the logic of halachah. The rabbis did not accept signs and miracles as proofs in legal arguments over Torah.[55] To satisfy his hosts, Jesus launched into a halachic discourse defending healing on the Sabbath day.

He asked them, "Which of you, having a son or an ox that has fallen into a well on a Sabbath day, will not immediately pull him out?" (Luke 14:5). As in Matthew 12, the question is rhetorical:[56]

> Which one of you who has a sheep, if it falls into a pit on the Sabbath, will not take hold of it and lift it out? Of how much more value is a man than a sheep! So it is lawful to do good on the Sabbath. (Matthew 12:11–12)

None of them would hesitate to violate the Sabbath in order to rescue one of their animals or children from a well on the Sabbath day.[57] In this instance, the argument asks: If it is permissible to violate Shabbat in order to immediately rescue a life or alleviate an animal's suffering, why should they postpone the infirm man's healing?

Apparently, the prominent Pharisee and his disciples accepted the Master's reasoning.

CONCLUSION TO THE SYNOPTIC SABBATH CONFLICTS

In the end, Jewish law came to similar conclusions as our Master, albeit by different lines of justification. Today, Jewish doctors are required to work over the Sabbath (when their duty shift dictates) without raising questions of Sabbath prohibitions. Theoretically, the potential for saving a life is always present when a doctor is on duty, but Jewish law now allows the Jewish doctor to conduct all medical procedures whether life is threatened or not—so long as he is on duty with the potential to save a life.

In the synoptic Gospels, Jesus based his argument for healing on the Sabbath primarily upon the rabbinic principle of *kal vachomer*, from the light to the heavy: "If it is permissible to violate Shabbat in order to do good to animals and alleviate their suffering, how much more so is it permissible to do the same for human beings?" These acts, though justifiable, still breach the Shabbat. Likewise, he justified the disciples' act of picking grain to alleviate their hunger on the same basis.

Jesus prioritized the alleviation of human suffering above the prohibitions of the Sabbath on the basis of Hosea 6:6: "For I desire steadfast love [mercy] and not sacrifice, the knowledge of God rather than burnt offerings." If picking and husking grain, healing a withered arm, lifting an ox out of a pit, and tethering and un-tethering an ox or donkey to lead it to water did not actually constitute legal violations of the Sabbath,[58] Jesus could have simply said so. He would not have needed to bother with a halachic justification that attempted to demonstrate why it should be permissible to violate the Sabbath in these instances.

For many Bible readers, this distinction may be too obscure, but if missed, the reader also misses the message of all the Sabbath stories in the Gospels. The essential message is not that Jesus has cancelled the Sabbath or that the rabbinic interpretation of Sabbath is illegitimate. The Sabbath-conflict stories instead communicate that acts of compassion and mercy performed to alleviate human suffering take precedence over the ritual taboo. The miraculous power by which Jesus performs the healings only serves to add God's endorsement to Jesus' halachic, legal rationale.

Did Jesus' disciples break the Sabbath in the grain fields? Yes. But they were justified in so doing because their need took precedence, just as the hunger of David and his men took precedence over the Temple service, and the Temple service took precedence over the Sabbath. Therefore Jesus declared them guiltless and told the Pharisees, "If you had known what this means, 'I desire mercy, and not sacrifice,' you would not have condemned the guiltless" (Matthew 12:7).

Did the Master break the Sabbath when he healed on the Sabbath day? Yes. Would fixing a car break the Sabbath? Of course it would, and by the same standard so does fixing a human body. Nevertheless, the Master justified doing so because compassion for his fellow man took precedence over the Sabbath.

Outside of this exception of doing good and offering compassion to alleviate human suffering, Jesus did not deem the aforementioned violations justifiable. If the disciples picked and husked the grain and carried it away in their pockets or threw it on the ground, they would have broken the Sabbath without justification. If Jesus decided to apply his healing power to cracked pottery, and if instead of healing human beings, he began to miraculously heal cracks in pottery on the Sabbath, just for the sake of repairing pottery, he would have been breaking the Sabbath without justification, because pots are not lord of the Sabbath, and the Sabbath was not made for pots.

The Son of Man who took such great delight in healing the afflictions of his fellow Jews on the holy Sabbath day thereby revealed the true nature of that day of redemption. He also revealed the true heart of the Father who made the Sabbath for man and not man for the Sabbath and who made man the lord of the Sabbath, that man should "call the Sabbath a delight and the holy day of the LORD honorable" (Isaiah 58:13).

PART TWO

Sabbath Conflicts in the Gospel of John

CHAPTER EIGHT

The Healing at Bethesda

JOHN 5

Once it happened that our Master was on his way to the Temple courts, passing through the colonnades that surround the pools of Bethesda. Here and there, the sick and disabled lay beside the pool, waiting for the miraculous stirring of the waters.

PICK UP YOUR MAT

Jesus stopped at the mat of one particular man, a paralytic who had not walked for thirty-eight years. In the race to reach the water first, he had an obvious disadvantage. The Master knew the man had waited a long time. Perhaps more than anyone else at the pool that day; he was a man without hope. The Master asked him, "Do want to be healed?" (John 5:6). The man had never seen Jesus before; he knew nothing about him. He did not realize that Jesus was offering him a healing. He explained, "Sir, I have no one to put me into the pool when the water is stirred up, and while I am going another steps down before me" (John 5:7).

The Master said, "Get up, take up your bed, and walk" (John 5:8). Before the man had time to consider whether or not he believed or had enough faith in the mysterious healer, he felt life and revivification pour into his limbs. He obeyed the stranger, stood up, and picked up the bedroll on which he had been lying. "Now that day was the Sabbath" (John 5:9).

CARRYING ON THE SABBATH

The Master tells the man to pick up his bedroll and carry it. Several men protested when they saw the healed man carrying his bedroll over his shoulder. Traditional Sabbath law prohibits a Jewish person from carrying an object in a public domain. Objects can be moved about and carried within a private home, courtyard, or pre-determined domain, but they cannot be carried from a private domain into a public space nor carried in public space. Practically speaking, this means that on the Sabbath day a Jewish person is not to carry an object more than four cubits outside his home.

Ordinarily, Christian readers dismiss the law against carrying an object on the Sabbath day as a rabbinic fiction. The interpretation of the law is part of Jewish tradition,[59] but the law itself is based squarely upon biblical text. The rule is derived from two principle passages of scripture:

> Remain each of you in his place; let no one go out of his place on the seventh day. (Exodus 16:29)

> Thus says the LORD: Take care for the sake of your lives, and do not bear a burden [carried thing] on the Sabbath day or bring it in by the gates of Jerusalem. And do not carry a burden [carried thing] out of your houses on the Sabbath or do any work, but keep the Sabbath day holy, as I commanded your fathers. (Jeremiah 17:21–22)

In addition, the Torah tells a story about a man who was found gathering and carrying sticks on the Sabbath day. Moses did not know what to do with the man. The LORD instructed the community to stone him to death for violating the Sabbath.[60]

The sages determined that "transferring an object from one domain to another" constitutes a violation of the Sabbath.[61] The rule allows a Jewish person carrying an object outside of a private domain to walk less than four cubits on the Sabbath. From that perspective, the carrying of the bedroll seems to violate the Sabbath.

The laws of carrying are extremely complex, and we do not know exactly how they were understood or practiced in the days of the Master. David Instone-Brewer believes that in the days of the Master, the prohibition on carrying had not yet fully developed and that the Pharisees who challenged the man with the mat may have been applying a rigid standard that had not yet been accepted by the populace.[62]

An early opinion in the Mishnah states: "One who carries a living person on a litter is not liable for carrying the litter because the litter is dependent upon the person being carried."[63] This law seems to imply that some opinions allowed for carrying another person on the Sabbath, even if the person was carried upon a bed. The same opinion, however, implies that if a person was not in the bed, the bed should not be carried.

As the man walked through the porticoes of Bethesda with his bedroll over his shoulder, several religious leaders challenged him, "It is the Sabbath, and it is not lawful for you to take up your bed" (John 5:10). The man quickly explained that he had been miraculously healed only moments earlier and that the man who healed him was the one who told him to pick up his mat and carry it. The man's explanation raised another concern. Who was going about and healing people on the Sabbath day?

The religious leaders asked him, "Who is the man who said to you, 'Take up your bed and walk'?" (John 5:12). The man did not know.

AN UNANSWERED QUESTION

The Gospel of John only uses the bedroll incident to explain why the Judean religious authorities took notice of the man at Bethesda. If they had not seen him carrying his bedroll, the entire healing miracle might have escaped their notice. The writer of John pays no further attention to the question of carrying on the Sabbath, and the matter is not raised again. That leaves the readers wondering, "Why did Jesus tell the man to pick up his bedroll and carry it?"

Surely our Master could have healed the man simply by telling him, "Stand up and walk." Was it necessary to also tell him to carry his mat?

We might suppose that he told him to carry his bedroll in order to make a public statement. Christian interpretation ordinarily assumes that Jesus wanted to prove to everyone that the Sabbath has been abolished. Hebrew-roots, Sabbatarian interpretations often assume that, while upholding the biblical Sabbath, Jesus demonstrated that the prohibition on carrying an object on the Sabbath is an unjustified rabbinic fiction. Perhaps by telling the man to carry his mat, Jesus demonstrated that carrying an object in a public space does not violate the Sabbath. If so, he was thereby encouraging people to throw off the rules of traditional Judaism and begin carrying objects around on the Sabbath.

This interpretation does not work. Jesus never did make any statements about carrying on the Sabbath. In John 5, he did not stay behind to defend the man or argue Sabbath halachah with the sages. Instead, Jesus slipped away from sight, fading into the crowd.[64] He did not attempt to correct their interpretation, and he offered no legal justification for carrying on the Sabbath.

He himself did not carry, nor did his prosecutors ever accuse him or any of his followers of carrying on the Sabbath. So why does he tell the man to carry his bedroll on the Sabbath?

To our great sorrow, the Gospel of John omits any explanation and shifts to focus on the question of whether or not Jesus is justified in healing on the Sabbath. John leaves the entire bedroll incident unexplained and unresolved. Nevertheless, we may still indulge in some speculation around the question.

A PUBLIC DOMAIN

In his Hebrew commentary on the New Testament, Rabbi Lichtenstein offers two attempts to explain the bedroll incident.[65] First, Lichtenstein cites a teaching of Rabbi Akiba. The wicked [Roman governor] Tinneus Rufus said to Rabbi Akiba, "If the Holy One, blessed be he, keeps the Sabbath, then he should not cause the winds to blow or cause the rain to fall on that day." Rabbi Akiba retorted, "A man is allowed to carry an object within his own private domain, and the whole universe belongs to God as his private domain."[66] Following Akiba's lead, Lichtenstein reasons that the private domain of a father also belongs to the son. Therefore the entire universe is the Son of God's private domain, and thus the Son of God may carry any object anyplace on the Sabbath without concern.

Lichtenstein's reasoning fails to satisfy. In the story, Jesus does not carry an object, but he tells the man to carry the object. Furthermore, if Jesus applied that reasoning, he could have likewise exempted himself from virtually any commandment normally incumbent upon a human being. For example, since God owns everything, Jesus could have felt justified in helping himself to other people's possessions. It would not be theft for him because everything is the LORD's. Likewise, he could take any woman since all Israel is the bride of God. Likewise, because God provides food for his creatures on the Sabbath day, Jesus could have justified cooking on the Sabbath. The list of possible divine prerogatives he might claim seems endless.

In reality, our Master never invoked divine privilege to exempt himself from rules incumbent upon "normal" human beings. Instead, "God sent forth his Son, born of a woman, born under the law" (Galatians 4:4). "Although he was a son, he learned obedience" (Hebrews 5:8). He "did not count equality with God a thing to be grasped" (Philippians 2:6).

A RECOGNIZED PROPHET

Rabbi Lichtenstein seems to have realized that his first explanation did not work because he immediately offered a second attempt. Still commenting on the same question, he points out that Talmudic law allows a recognized prophet to override a prohibition of the Torah in order to meet an urgent need of the moment. The Talmud cites the example of Elijah the prophet who built an altar and offered a sacrifice outside of Jerusalem in order to thwart the prophets of Baal.

> Come and learn. [The Torah says in Deuteronomy 18:15, "The LORD your God will raise up for you a prophet like me from among you, from your countrymen,] you shall listen to him." You must listen to him even if the prophet tells you to transgress one of the commandments of the Torah, as Elijah did on Mount Carmel. Every case must be weighed according to the needs of the situation. (b. *Yavamot* 90b)

In other words, the extenuating circumstances warranted Elijah's temporary transgression of the ritual concern. Since the people of Israel knew that Elijah was a true prophet, they were required to listen to him, even though it seemed that he was violating a commandment. The sages extended this rule of prophetic authority only to a known, verified, and established prophet and only in situations in which the extenuating circumstances warranted the temporary suspension of a prohibition.[67]

Lichtenstein suggests that Jesus likewise had the authority to suspend temporarily the prohibition on carrying an object in public on a Sabbath day in order to meet the need of the hour. Just as Elijah had the authority to set aside the prohibition on sacrificing outside of the Temple in Jerusalem, Jesus had the authority to tell the man to carry his bedroll.

Again, Lichtenstein's explanation fails to satisfy. Jesus was not an established and known prophet yet. He was a complete stranger to the man he healed. The Pharisees who later interviewed him may have heard of him before, but they did not yet know him as a reputable prophet. Moreover, Jesus offered no rationalization to explain why the demands of the hour necessitated temporarily setting the prohibition aside. Neither are any extenuating circumstances that might warrant the temporary suspension of Sabbath law self-evident in the story.

Rabbi Lichtenstein deserves credit for his two attempts to answer the problem from within halachic discourse, but neither answer seems sufficient.

WITHIN THE ERUV

In his *Jewish New Testament Commentary*, David Stern suggests that the problem was simply a disagreement over what constituted a proper *eruv* (עירוב). As mentioned earlier, Sabbath law allows a Jewish person to carry an object within his own domain, but he can only carry an object a distance of less than four cubits in a public domain. In order to alleviate the restriction, the sages devised a way for members of a community to join their homes, courtyards, and neighborhood into one large, common domain legally. Prior to the Sabbath, the community needed to agree on the borders (*eruv*, עֵרוּב) of their shared domain and mark them off. By marking off a circumference around a common domain prior to the onset of the Sabbath and making a communal declaration of shared property within that circumference for the duration of the Sabbath, the community could legally declare a whole village or city as one common domain. So long as one was within the limits of the *eruv*-border, he was free to carry certain objects as if he was in his own home.[68]

The laws are complex. Based upon the prohibition of carrying a burden out of one's home on the Sabbath (Jeremiah 17:21–22), Jewish law considers it a biblical prohibition to carry an object on the Sabbath within a public domain or to carry from a private domain into a public domain. A third category of domain, a *karmelit*, is not quite public and not quite private. Most communal spaces belong in this category. Jewish law considers it biblically permissible to carry within a *karmelit*, to carry from one private domain to another, and to carry between a *karmelit* and a private domain. However, the features that distinguish between a *karmelit* and a public domain are complex and subtle. The sages felt that they were too easy to take for granted, so they made a rabbinic prohibition decreeing that carrying in a *karmelit*, carrying between a *karmelit* and a private domain, and carrying from one private domain to another are prohibited. These more stringent prohibitions are regarded as a rabbinic fence around the biblical commandment. A public domain is a public domain *de facto* and cannot be declared a private domain *de jure*. An *eruv* cannot ever be declared in a public domain. Therefore, the law of *eruv* alleviates the rabbinic prohibition, not a Torah prohibition. The *eruv* allows for leniency in the rabbinic law in the specific conditions in which people are intentional and educated about the situation and laws.

Stern argues that, as a walled city, all of Jerusalem was within the Sabbath *eruv*, and by Pharisaic law, carrying should have been permitted within the city. He assumes that the pool of Bethesda lay within the walls of Jerusalem and therefore within the *eruv*. Stern suggests that the Pharisees suspected the man was about to leave the *eruv* while carrying his mat.[69]

Stern's suggestion does not satisfy either. Why did Jesus not simply explain to his critics, "We were within the *eruv* when I told him to carry his mat"? Stern is also making an assumption about the wall line of Jerusalem in the days of the Master. According to most reconstructions of the walls of Jerusalem in those days, the pool of Bethesda was still outside the city walls, outside the Sheep Gate. A few decades later, King Herod Agrippa expanded the city and brought Bethesda inside the walls, but in the days of the Master, the pool remained outside the walls and hence outside the *eruv*. The pool of Bethesda may have been considered *karmelit*, but it was certainly not within Jerusalem's walls in the days of the Master.

MERCY, NOT SACRIFICE

Many believers assume that the story of the man carrying the mat on the Sabbath is evidence that Jesus disagreed with the interpretation of the laws that forbid carrying on Sabbath. Even if that were the case, it does not adequately explain why the Master told the man to pick up his mat and walk. Why make the unfortunate, paralytic man into a pawn in a halachic debate?

Arguing about the laws of carrying or what constitutes a proper *eruv* seems out of character for our Master. We never see him intentionally overturning Jewish tradition unless he has a sound reason for doing so, and when he does, he always states the reason. Entering an argument about whether or not a man is permitted to carry a particular object on the Sabbath seems beneath his dignity and outside the scope of his concern. It seems like an argument that Jesus would avoid because it fails to address "the weightier matters of the law: justice and mercy and faithfulness" (Matthew 23:23).

As mentioned above, other stories about Jesus healing on the Sabbath always point toward the weightier provisions of Torah. In those stories, the Master justifies violating the Sabbath for the sake of alleviating human suffering on the basis of a passage from Hosea 6:6: "If you had known what this means, 'I desire mercy, and not sacrifice,' you would not have condemned the guiltless" (Matthew 12:7). He used the passage to teach that compassion for human beings, specifically the alleviation of human suffering, takes precedence over ceremonial concern. The Hebrew word from Hosea 6:6 translated as "mercy" is *chesed* (חסד): "loving-kindness," "compassion," and "acts of love." Is there some way in which allowing the paralytic to carry his bedroll could be understood as an act of *chesed*?

RIGHTEOUSNESS BEFORE THE LORD

We may safely assume that after thirty-eight years of paralysis, the man at Bethesda had no other possession to his name other than the bedroll upon which he slept. The Torah shows special concern for just such a situation.

A passage in Deuteronomy creates a hypothetical scenario in which a poor man must secure a loan from a creditor. The poor man has nothing to offer for collateral except his cloak which also doubles as his bedroll. The Torah warns the creditor not to keep the collateral overnight. The creditor must return the man's cloak before sunset so that he will be able to sleep in it. If the creditor will do so, the LORD will reckon his act of mercy on the man as righteousness:

> When you make your neighbor a loan of any sort, ... if he is a poor man, you shall not sleep in his pledge. You shall restore to him the pledge as the sun sets, that he may sleep in his cloak and bless you. And it will be righteousness for you before the LORD your God. (Deuteronomy 24:10–13)

In John 5, the sick man's bed is equivalent to the poor man's cloak. Would our Master have told the man, "Get up and walk, but abandon your mat here because today is the Sabbath"? Would that not have violated the spirit of Deuteronomy 24:10–13?

Jesus prioritized mercy (*chesed*) above ceremonial concern and told the man to get up, go, and take his mat with him. In so doing, Jesus did not abrogate the prohibition on carrying on the Sabbath or declare that prohibition illegitimate. Neither did he criticize Jewish tradition about the Sabbath. Instead, he acted according to a higher ethical standard that says mercy on a human being overrides ceremonial prohibitions when necessary. Even according to strict rabbinic law, human dignity should take precedence. He summarizes this ethical override with the words, "The Sabbath was made for man, and not man for the Sabbath" (Mark 2:27).

This is especially so in the case of rabbinic prohibitions (stringencies, fences). Judaism teaches that any rabbinic decree can be justifiably violated for the sake of human dignity (*kevod haBeri'ot*). Some of the laws of carrying on the Sabbath apply on the level of Torah prohibition, whereas others apply only on the level of rabbinic decree (*d'rabbanan*). According to traditional Jewish law, the types of carrying that are merely rabbinic fences can be violated, when necessary, for the sake of human dignity. In this case, even though it was outside the line of the city walls, the area of the pool of Bethesda should have been considered *karmelit* (neither completely public nor completely private domain), an area in which carrying on the Sabbath could be permitted. Evidently, the authorities chose not to allow carrying in that area, perhaps because they could not agree on the exact legal parameters outside the walls, or perhaps in order to prevent people from taking the prohibitions on carrying lightly. If this is so, carrying within the area of the pool of Bethesda was only a rabbinic prohibition that should have been lifted in a case of preserving human dignity.[70] The Talmud contains many other examples in which human dignity is an issue in other contexts, sometimes even arguably overriding blatant Torah law, let alone rabbinic stringencies.

JEWISH BELIEVERS AND THE LAWS OF CARRYING

Jesus showed mercy to the sick man with the bedroll as an exception to the prohibition against carrying. He did not intend to set a new, lower standard by which he allowed his followers to disregard Sabbath law. Aside from the story in John 5, his opponents never accused him, his disciples, or his followers of ever carrying an object on the Sabbath. If the Master and his followers routinely broke that law, their opponents would have had ammunition for criticism and legal grounds to prosecute them as Sabbath breakers.

Neither the Gospels nor the rest of the New Testament indicates that Jesus or his followers began to carry objects in public domains on the Sabbath. On the contrary, our Master told his disciples, "Pray that your flight will not be ... on a Sabbath" (Matthew 24:20). Why? Sabbath law allows a person to break the Sabbath to save his life.[71]

Flight from enemies is permissible on the Sabbath for the sake of saving one's life, but the immediate threat to life does not justify carrying one's personal possessions. A man's life is not at stake if he leaves his bedroll and money belt behind him on the Sabbath day. Perhaps the Master tells his disciples to pray that they will not have to flee on the Sabbath so that they will not have to leave their possessions behind.[72]

CHAPTER NINE

The Mystical Answer

JOHN 5:14–47

Sometime later that same day, Jesus saw the man in the Temple. Apparently he had deposited his bedroll someplace and then gone up to the Temple to offer thanks to God.

The Master congratulated him on his healing and offered him a word of gospel: "Sin no more, that nothing worse may happen to you" (John 5:14). The man left and told the religious authorities the name of the one who had healed him: Jesus of Nazareth. The healed man intended no malice. He was not informing on the Master; Jesus never told him to keep his identity private. The man may have felt that he was honoring Jesus by reporting his name. The Pharisees who had rebuked the man for carrying the bedroll came to challenge Jesus about the matter of healing on the Sabbath day.[73] Their inquiry ignites the Master's first confrontation with the religious establishment of his day.

As soon as the Judean leadership was able to verify that Jesus was healing on the Sabbath, they harried him over the issue. They cornered him in the Temple courts and asked for some explanations.

As stated above, most of the rabbis of that day believed that healing constituted a form of "work" forbidden on the Sabbath. Jesus did not disagree with the opinion. Instead, he justified the work he did on the Sabbath with two different arguments. The first defense employs a philosophical and mystical answer, and appears in his dissertation in John 5. The second argument employs a halachic justification for healing on the Sabbath, and it appears in his dissertation in John 7. We will examine that argument in the next chapter.

IMITATING GOD

In John 5:17, Jesus explained why he felt justified performing acts of healing on the Sabbath: "My Father is working until now, and I am working."

Though God rested on the seventh day from the work of creating the universe, he did not rest from all forms of work. A similar teaching in the *Midrash Rabbah* depicts God working on the Sabbath to punish the wicked and reward the righteous:

> Rabbi Pinchas said in Rabbi Oshaya's name, "In the Torah it says, '[By the seventh day God] completed his work which he had done, [and he rested on the seventh day from all his work].' He rested only from the work of creating his world, but not from the work of [dealing with] the wicked and the work [of dealing with] the righteous, for he works with the former and with the latter. He shows the wicked their true nature, and the righteous their true nature ... the punishment of the wicked is called work ... bestowing the reward of the righteous is called work. (*Genesis Rabbah* 11:10)

The *Midrash Rabbah* also mentions that God causes wind to blow and rain to fall even on the Sabbath.[74] Aside from resting from the work of creation, God continues with all other forms of "God-work" even on the Sabbath day.

Our Master argues that God continued to do the work of redemption even after the sixth day of creation. Until the ultimate and final Sabbath when redemption is complete, God will not rest from that labor. Until that day when there is no more sickness, suffering, or sin, the Father continues to work among men. In the same way, Jesus does the work of redemption even on the Sabbath.

Whether he is ordering the universe, stirring the winds, punishing the wicked, rewarding the righteous, or healing the sick, God receives an exemption from ceasing on the Sabbath. Jesus claims that since he is doing the work of his father (i.e., redemption, healing), he enjoys the same exemption.

EQUAL WITH GOD

Our Master justified healing on the Sabbath by saying, "My Father is working until now, and I am working" (John 5:17). The religious leaders misunderstood. They thought he was claiming to be on the same par with God. They reduced his argument to mean, "If God can break the Sabbath, then I can break the Sabbath because I have the same privileges as God." They thought that because he claimed the same rights as God, he claimed to be equal with God.[75]

Was Jesus claiming divine exemption from the Sabbath on the basis that he was equal with God? Or did the religious leaders misunderstand him? Would the Gospel of John present Jesus as God's equal? Christian theology teaches that the Son is equal to the Father in regard to his divinity but subordinate to the Father in regard to his humanity.[76] "However, the NT view of the relationship is primarily from the viewpoint of the humanity of the Son."[77] Paul teaches that Jesus "did not count equality with God a thing to be grasped" (Philippians 2:6), and John 14:28 reports Jesus saying, "The Father is greater than I."

Jesus is the Logos made flesh, in whom the fullness of God dwells in bodily form, but that was not his point as he tried to explain why he felt free to heal on the Sabbath. He never justified his actions with the argument, "I'm God in the flesh; therefore, I can do whatever I want."

Instead, the Master argued that God performs certain labors on the Sabbath day because they take priority over the Sabbath. For example, God causes the wind to blow and the rain to fall on the Sabbath because sustaining the natural order takes precedence over the Sabbath. So too God heals and saves on the Sabbath because human lives take precedence over the Sabbath. Jesus justified healing the man on the Sabbath because it is the kind of work which the Father has been doing since the six days of creation.

THE PARABLE OF THE APPRENTICE

> So Jesus said to them, "Truly, truly, I say to you, the Son can do nothing of his own accord, but only what he sees the Father doing. For whatever the Father does, that the Son does likewise. For the Father loves the Son and shows him all that he himself is doing. And greater works than these will he show him, so that you may marvel." (John 5:19–20)

The Judeans who hassled the Master about healing on the Sabbath misunderstood his explanation. They thought that, by referring to himself as the Son and to God as his Father, Jesus claimed that he had the right to work on the Sabbath because he was equal with God.

He then attempted to explain more clearly by comparing himself to a boy apprenticed in a trade by his father.[78] C.H. Dodd suggests that John 5:19–20 is just the summary of a parable that Jesus told to explain his own relationship to God in terms of a son's apprenticeship under his father.[79] If there ever was such a parable, the writer of the Gospel of John reduced it to its essential message: The Father teaches the Son his work, and the Son learns his work from the Father.

The original parable may have sounded like this:

> To what can it be compared? It can be compared to a man who wanted his son to take up a trade, but the son did not know how to do anything by himself. The man said, "I love my son and want him to be able to provide for himself. I will bring him to work with me and show him how to do everything I do." The son watched his father at work, and he learned to do all that his father could do. Soon the son could do whatever he saw his father doing. Whatever the man did, the son also learned to do. "Truly, truly, I say to you, the Son can do nothing of himself, unless it is something he sees the Father doing."

THE PARABLE OF THE FATHER'S APPRENTICE
(JOHN 5:19–20)

The father = God

The son = Jesus

The father's trade = the work of redemption (such as healing, even on the Sabbath)

The apprenticeship = Jesus' imitation of God

Meaning = Jesus heals on the Sabbath as an act of imitating God.

The parable evokes scenes from the carpenter shop in Nazareth. Just as Jesus learned the carpentry trade from watching his father Joseph, so too he learned his healing trade from observing his Father in heaven. Since God heals and saves on the Sabbath, his apprentice does so as well.

Jesus argued that he heals on the Sabbath primarily as a matter of imitating God. The principle of imitating God is at the core of all Jewish ethics:[80]

> Just as the Holy One, blessed be he, is called Merciful, so should you be merciful, just as he is called Gracious, so should you be gracious, just as he is called Righteous, so should you be righteous; just as he is called devout, so should you be a devout one. (*Sifre* on Deuteronomy 10:12)

Jesus performed works of healing that he learned to do from observing his Father in heaven. He told his critics that he anticipated learning even greater works from his Father in the future. He said, "The Father will show [me] greater works than these, so that you will marvel," which is to say, "You have not see anything yet." They will marvel at the works God gives his Son to accomplish.

CHAPTER TEN

The Halachic Answer

JOHN 7:21–24

> If on the Sabbath a man receives circumcision, so that the law of Moses may not be broken, are you angry with me because on the Sabbath I made a man's whole body well? Do not judge by appearances, but judge with right judgment. (John 7:23–24)

Why did some of the Pharisees and the sages want the Master dead? Jesus recognized that his trouble with the sages in Jerusalem first began when he healed the disabled man at the Pool of Bethesda.[81] "I did one work, and you all marvel" he said (John 7:21). That "one work" had garnered the resentment of some prominent sages. "And this was why the Jews [religious authorities] were persecuting Jesus, because he was doing these things on the Sabbath" (John 5:16). No doubt, rumors of other Sabbath-day healings in Galilee had reached their ears as well. After one Sabbath-day healing in a Galilean synagogue, the Galilean Pharisees present that day "held counsel with the Herodians against him, how to destroy him" (Mark 3:6).

After the healing beside the pools of Bethesda, the Master discussed the matter with the Judean Pharisees who objected to his blatant violation of Sabbath prohibitions. In that first conversation regarding the question of healing on the Sabbath, Jesus attempted to justify his action with a mystical and eschatological argument which depended heavily on his cryptic self-identity as the Son of

Man.[82] That discussion had not gone well. The Master attempted to return to that conversation and redress his initial argument about healing on the Sabbath with a halachic approach. Jesus reasoned from the light to the heavy (*kal vachomer*, קל וחומר):[83]

> Moses gave you circumcision (not that it is from Moses, but from the fathers), and you circumcise a man on the Sabbath. If on the Sabbath a man receives circumcision, so that the law of Moses may not be broken, are you angry with me because on the Sabbath I made a man's whole body well? Do not judge by appearances, but judge with right judgment. (John 7:22–24)

Circumcision is a surgical, even medical, procedure. It constitutes a form of work (*melachah*) forbidden on the Shabbat. The Torah, however, mandates that a baby boy must be circumcised on the eighth day. When a woman gives birth to a son on the Sabbath day, a contradiction arises. The eighth day will also be a Shabbat. On the one hand, the Torah commands the family to "do no work," but on the other hand, the Torah commands the family to perform an act of *melachah* by circumcising the infant on that specific day. Which commandment takes precedence? According to the sages, a positive commandment takes precedence over a prohibition.

> Wherever you find a positive commandment and a negative commandment contradicting, if you can fulfill both of them, it is preferable, but if not, let the positive command come and supersede the negative command. (b.*Shabbat* 133a)

The sages agreed that the positive commandment to circumcise on the eighth day supersedes the prohibition against *melachah* on the Sabbath.[84] Whenever the eighth day falls on a Sabbath, the family of the child must set aside the Sabbath prohibition and perform the circumcision. Rabbi Yosi said, "Great is circumcision, since it overrides the prohibition of the Sabbath, which is subject to strict regulations."[85]

The rabbis considered the surgical procedure of circumcision as medical correction, an improvement to the body. Rabbi Yehudah observed, "Despite all the commandments which Abraham our father observed, he was called complete and whole only when he had circumcised himself, as it says [in Genesis 17:1], 'Walk before me, and be blameless.'"

Jesus reasoned, "If it is then permissible to make a medical adjustment to one small part of the body to correct it, how much more so should it be permissible to make a medical adjustment to correct the rest of the body." The Master's logic follows a simple line of halachic reasoning:

1. A surgical procedure constitutes *melachah* forbidden on Sabbath.
2. Circumcision is a surgical procedure and should, therefore, not occur on Sabbath.
3. Yet the commandment to circumcise supersedes the Sabbath prohibition.
4. Circumcision is a surgical procedure performed for the sake of only one body part.
5. Therefore the healing of a man's whole body should supersede the Sabbath more so.

He employs the same line of reasoning when he asks the Pharisees, "Have you not read in the Law how on the Sabbath the priests in the temple profane the Sabbath and are guiltless?" (Matthew 12:5).[86] In other words, there are situations in which the Torah requires us to violate the Sabbath:

> Lest one suppose that circumcision or the Temple service or a potential loss of life [are subject to the prohibitions of the Sabbath], the Scriptures make a distinction … There are times that you must rest on the Sabbath, and times that you must not rest on the Sabbath. Rabbi Eliezer says, "As to circumcision, why do they allow it to supersede the prohibitions on the Sabbath? It is because they are liable to being cut off [from Israel] if it is not accomplished at the proper time. Now behold, this can be argued from the light to the heavy (*kal vachomer*). If they override the Sabbath on account of a single member of the body, how much more should they override the prohibitions of the Sabbath to save the whole body?" (t.*Shabbat* 15:16)

The sages agreed with Jesus' reasoning up to a point. Rabbi Eliezer, a disciple of Yochanan ben Zakkai, may have heard the Master's conversation that day with the sages and derived his argument from Jesus. As Rabbi Eliezer articulates in the argument above, the Sabbath should certainly be set aside for the sake of saving a life, even if the threat to life is uncertain. Eliezer did not go so far as to say that the Sabbath should be set aside to heal a person even when no threat to life is present. "The principles drawn from the practice of circumcision on the Sabbath refer only to cases where life is in immediate danger. This condition was not satisfied in the Sabbath healings recorded in the Gospels, certainly not in [John] 5:1–9; a man who had waited 38 years might well have waited one more day."[87] Lichtenstein explains, "And there are several instances in which he healed the sick on the Sabbath. For the thinking of Jesus was that even when life is not in danger (that is, in immediate danger), it is permitted to heal on the Sabbath."[88]

Notice that Jesus' argument falls apart if he did not believe that healing constitutes a legitimate violation of the Sabbath prohibitions. If he believed that healing did not fall into the category of "work" (*melachah*) forbidden on the Sabbath, he should have framed the argument completely differently. Instead, his argument assumes that circumcision is a legitimate violation of Sabbath, and yet the Torah requires it to take place on the Sabbath. Likewise, the argument assumes that healing—even miraculous healing—breaks the Sabbath prohibitions, yet the priority of compassion for human beings requires it.

As noted above from Eliezer's argument in the Tosefta, Jesus' halachic argument was so cogent and well-reasoned that the sages themselves seem to have adopted it for application in cases that involved a potential threat to life:

> Rabbi Eleazar [ben Azariah] answered, "If circumcision, which involves a remedy for only one of the 248 parts of the human body, supersedes the Sabbath, how much more does saving the whole body supersede the Sabbath!" (b. *Yoma* 85b)

The rabbis commonly engaged in this type of halachic reasoning in their disputations. They did so to keep the sacred charge

Moses issued to the judges and legislators: "Judge the people with righteous judgment" (Deuteronomy 16:18). The Great Assembly of Ezra's generation reiterated the charge: "Be deliberate in judgment."[89] Jesus reminded his colleagues of that responsibility when he concluded his halachic argument with an allusion to Deuteronomy 16:18, "Do not judge by appearances, but judge with right judgment" (John 7:24).

CHAPTER ELEVEN

Healing the Blind Man

JOHN 9:1–16

The Master and his disciples encountered a man blind from birth. He spat on the ground, made mud of the spittle, and applied the mud to the man's eyes. Then he told the man, "Go, wash in the pool of Siloam." The man went and immersed, and miraculously, he could see. "Now it was a Sabbath day when Jesus made the mud and opened his eyes" (John 9:14).

MUD AND SPITTLE

The Master's other healings demonstrate that none of this was necessary. He could have just touched the man, or he even might have spoken a single word to open the man's unseeing eyes. Jesus ordinarily healed men and women in a purely supernatural manner. Why the elaborate concoction this time?

As pointed out in the introduction to this book, this single healing incident from the Gospels potentially involves three Sabbath violations. To heal the man, Jesus spat on the ground and made mud out of the spittle and the earth. Mixing two substances to form a third is a form of work prohibited on the Sabbath day. Mixing two substances together into a third falls under the prohibition of kneading.[90] It is *melachah* (מלאכה). It is making.

First-century Jewish folk medicine considered spittle a remedy for eye trouble, particularly the spittle of a firstborn son.[91] Jesus mixed his spittle with the dirt of the ground to make mud. He then applied the mud/saliva mixture to the man's eyes as a salve. Applying a salve or medicine by means of smearing is also considered a form of work prohibited on the Sabbath day. It is a form of *melachah*, a violation of the Sabbath. The application of spittle to the eyes on Shabbat is expressly forbidden in the Jerusalem Talmud.[92]

He sent the man to immerse himself. At least by conventional definition of Sabbath law, Jews do not immerse on the Sabbath.

Our Master's enemies declared, "This man is not from God, for he does not keep the Sabbath" (John 9:16). They wanted to prove that Jesus of Nazareth broke the Sabbath and taught others to do so as well. According to the Torah, breaking the Sabbath is a sin for a Jew. If they could prove that he was a sinner and that he condoned sin, they could prove that he was not the Messiah.

A TALMUDIC DEBATE

A discussion from the Talmud illustrates the issues at hand in the story of the blind man of John 9. The rabbis argue about whether or not an eye condition is serious enough to warrant setting aside the Sabbath prohibition in order to apply a medical salve. According to one opinion, the salve could be applied only if someone had already prepared and brought the herbal medicines prior to the Sabbath:

> Rabbi Zutra bar Toviah said in the name of Rav: "An eye that is irritated, it is permissible to apply salve to the eye on the Sabbath. Rav was understood to be of opinion that it is only permissible when the medicine for the salve had been ground the previous day, but if it is necessary to grind them on the Sabbath and carry them in public, it would not be permissible." (b.*Avodah Zarah* 28b)

A second opinion states that grinding the medicines and carrying them on the Sabbath is permissible for the sake of treating an inflamed eye:

> But one of the rabbis, Rabbi Yaakov, contradicted him saying, "It was taught to me according to Rav Yehudah that even grinding on the Sabbath and the carrying through

the public street are permissible." Rav Yehudah declared it as permissible to apply salve to the eye on the Sabbath. (b.*Avodah Zarah* 28b)

Not everyone agreed with this second opinion. Rabbi Shmuel bar Yehudah said, "Anyone who acts according to Yehudah's opinion breaks the Sabbath!" Ironically, sometime later, Shmuel suffered from an inflamed eye on the Sabbath. He asked Rav Yehudah if treating his eye on the Sabbath was permissible or forbidden. Rav Yehudah replied, "For everyone else it is permitted—but for you it is forbidden."

Rav Yehudah told a story about why preparing and administering medicine for a sore eye should be permitted even on the Sabbath:

> It once happened to a maidservant in Mar Shmuel's house that her eye became inflamed on a Sabbath. She cried, but no one attended her [because of the Sabbath prohibitions] and her eye burst. The very next day, Mar Shmuel went out and taught that if one's eye gets out of order it is permissible to apply salve even on the Sabbath." (b.*Avodah Zarah* 28b)

The Talmud goes on to justify Sabbath-day eye treatments on the basis that an inflamed eye might cause a threat to one's life. "What is the reason it is permitted?" the sages asked. "Because the eyesight is connected with the muscles of the heart." In other words, the eye condition might develop into a more serious matter which constitutes a threat to life, and therefore its treatment takes precedence over the Sabbath as matter of saving a life. Nevertheless, all agreed that this exception to the rule did not apply to a preexisting condition, nor could medicine be prepared and applied to an eye on the Sabbath simply to improve one's vision.

HALACHAH OF JESUS

Had Jesus been party to the above conversation, he would have disagreed with the final ruling. As we saw in the synoptic Sabbath conflicts, Rabbi Jesus believed that compassion for human beings takes precedence over Sabbath prohibitions, even when a man's malady or disability poses no immediate threat to life. He taught that, since the Sabbath is made for man and not man for the Sabbath, the alleviation of human suffering supersedes the Sabbath prohibitions.

As explained earlier in this booklet, Jesus often used the Hosea 6:6 passage to teach that compassion for human beings takes precedence over ceremonial concern. For example, when the Pharisees criticized him for eating and drinking with sinners and tax collectors, he quoted Hosea 6:6 to justify his choice of table fellowship. He explained that he chose to associate with sinners because, like a physician caring for a sick patient, he sought to alleviate their spiritual sickness:

> But when he heard it, he said, "Those who are well have no need of a physician, but those who are sick. Go and learn what this means, 'I desire mercy, and not sacrifice.' For I came not to call the righteous, but sinners." (Matthew 9:12–13)

The Hebrew word from Hosea 6:6 translated as "mercy" is *chesed* (חסד), which, in Judaism, is generally understood to mean loving-kindness, compassion, and acts of love.

> For I desire steadfast love [mercy] and not sacrifice, the knowledge of God rather than burnt offerings. (Hosea 6:6)

Jesus reminded the rabbis of his day that the Temple service, with its sacrifices and burnt offerings, takes priority over the Sabbath.[93] Since *chesed* should take priority over the Temple sacrifices, and the Temple sacrifices take priority over the Sabbath, then *chesed* must also take priority over the Sabbath.

In the synoptic Gospels, Jesus' argument for healing on the Sabbath is based primarily upon the rabbinic principle of *kal vachomer*, from the light to the heavy. "If it is permissible to violate Shabbat in order to do good to animals and alleviate their suffering, how much more so is it permissible to do the same for human beings?" These acts, though justifiable, still breach the Shabbat.

The essential message is not that Jesus has cancelled the Sabbath, or that the rabbinic interpretation of Sabbath is illegitimate. The message is that acts of compassion and mercy performed to alleviate human suffering take precedence over the Sabbath's prohibitions. The miraculous power by which Jesus performs the healings only serves to add God's endorsement to Jesus' legal rationale.

PRACTICING MEDICINE ON THE SABBATH

This explains why the Master used the spittle, the mud, and the immersion to heal the blind man on the Sabbath. As mentioned above, he could have dispensed with all of that and simply touched the man's eyes or spoken a word to heal him. Instead, he chose to apply a medical treatment such as a first-century doctor might have done. He chose to deliberately step over the boundaries of Sabbath law for the sake of healing the man, and he chose to do so in a manner that any disciple of his might emulate.

In so doing, Jesus provided a model for his disciples. If he had never used a conventional, medical means to heal on the Sabbath, we might have supposed that Sabbath-day healings are permissible only so long as they are of a completely miraculous nature. By making the mud, smearing it on the man's eyes, and telling him to wash it out of his eyes, the Master demonstrated that one may prepare and administer medical treatments on the Sabbath even if they are not miraculous.

Christian Sabbatarians object; they ask, "Where in the Bible does it say that mixing mud and applying salve violate the Sabbath?" They contend, "Jesus did these things to demonstrate that such actions are not a violation of the Sabbath."

This logic falls apart when the healing of the blind man is compared with similar Sabbath-conflict stories in the synoptic Gospels. In every instance, Jesus offered a halachic justification for why the healing overrides the prohibitions of the Sabbath. He never said, "Do you not realize that healing is not a violation of the Sabbath?" Instead, he always assumed that the miraculous healing he had performed had broken the Sabbath, but he justified breaking the Sabbath because compassion for human beings supersedes ritual concern. If Jesus admitted that a miraculous healing constituted an act of *melachah* ordinarily prohibited on Sabbath, how much more so does an act of conventional healing?

PART THREE

The Thirty-Nine Prohibited Forms of Work

CHAPTER TWELVE

The Thirty-Nine Forms of Work

MISHNAH SHABBAT 7:2

What does it mean to work on the Sabbath day? From what, exactly, are Sabbath keepers supposed to rest? The sages answered that question by conducting a careful Torah study on the construction of the Tabernacle at Mount Sinai.

Before instructing the people of Israel about the work (*melachah*, מלאכה) of the Tabernacle, Moses first enjoined them not to do any work (*melachah*) on the Sabbath day. Naturally, the Israelites would have assumed that it was permissible to work on the Sabbath as long as they were working for the holy purpose of building the Sanctuary. It seems a reasonable conclusion. As long as one does holy work, that work must be permissible on the Sabbath, right? In some cases this logic holds true. For example, the priesthood worked on the Sabbath by carrying out the sacrificial services and the divine worship on the Sabbath day. As we have seen, our Master stated, "On the Sabbath the priests in the temple profane the Sabbath and are guiltless" (Matthew 12:5). A person might logically infer, therefore, that all work connected with the Sanctuary is exempt from the Sabbath prohibition. Therefore, the Torah explicitly juxtaposes the Sabbath prohibition on *melachah* with the description of the *melachah* involved in building the Tabernacle to teach that it is not permissible to break the Sabbath for the sake of building the Sanctuary.

What exactly constitutes prohibited work, and what does not? English readers mistakenly assume that the Sabbath's prohibition on "work" applies to the English-speaker's definitions of the word "work." People often think that the type of "work" prohibited on the Sabbath involves heavy physical labor. Others might suppose that the Sabbath prohibits only vocational work, i.e., one's job or career. As explained in the first chapter, the Hebrew word *melachah* (מלאכה), which our English Bibles translate as "work," does not necessarily mean one's vocation, nor does it mean hard labor.

The English language contains no equivalent for the word *melachah*, but the creation narrative in Genesis provides a contextual meaning which defines it as creative acts of production including the creation of light, the creation of substance, formation, separation, planting, and creative activities of making, mixing, shaping, and altering. Any act that takes mastery of creation, therefore, might be considered to be a form of *melachah*.

THE TABERNACLE

The judges and sages of Israel needed to delineate their definition of *melachah* tightly because the Torah says, "Whoever does any *melachah* on it shall be put to death." The Sanhedrin was responsible for prosecuting Sabbath breakers, therefore, they needed a concrete, standardized definition of *melachah*. They found it in the Torah portion in which the Torah forbids *melachah* on the Sabbath day and then refers to the labors involved in creating the Tabernacle as various forms of *melachah*.

The Sabbath prohibitions of Exodus 31 and 35 pertain directly to the *melachah* of the Tabernacle: "Whoever does any *melachah* on it, that soul shall be cut off from among his people" (31:14), and "whoever does any *melachah* on it shall be put to death" (35:2).

The Torah also says (just a few verses before the Sabbath prohibition in Exodus 31 and shortly after the prohibition of 35) that Bezalel and Oholiab were "skilled in all kinds of *melachah*" (Exodus 31:2–6).

Obviously, *melachah* is not just physically intensive labor or vocational work. It involves the work of shaping, creating, and making things—production which might be regarded as skills, hobbies, and crafts. It includes recreational, relaxing types of things like working in a garden or spending an afternoon doing needlework. Someone might object, "Why should I be prohibited from engaging in things that I enjoy on the Sabbath day?" This objection misses the point. God probably enjoyed creating the heavens and the earth. A religious Jew desists from *melachah* on the Sabbath day because God commands him to do so, not because he dislikes *melachah*. *Melachah* is not the opposite of "play" or leisure.

MASTERY OVER NATURE

Melachah involves taking mastery over nature to alter it in some fashion. The original *melachah* from which God rested when He first instituted the Sabbath involved shaping, creating, forming, making, ordering, structuring, organizing, separating, mixing, and molding things to produce results. He rested from imposing will onto substance and from creating order from disorder. He rested from producing.

This explains why Exodus 16:23 prohibits cooking, boiling, and baking on the Sabbath; those things involve "making" food as part of a production process, changing one substance into another substance. Sabbath-observant people cook their meals prior to the Sabbath, not on Sabbath: "This is what the LORD has commanded: 'Tomorrow is a day of solemn rest, a holy Sabbath to the LORD; bake what you will bake and boil what you will boil, and all that is left over lay aside to be kept till the morning'" (Exodus 16:23).

On the Sabbath we are to rest from making things, but the distinctions between making and not making are not always self-evident. For example, pouring milk on cold cereal is not making the cereal, but cooking oatmeal in a pot is making the cereal and constitutes *melachah*. Therefore Jewish law deems it permissible to keep pre-cooked food warm but not to cook it on the Sabbath.

On the Sabbath, we rest from imposing our will; we rest from restructuring, reordering, and making things. Even gathering is prohibited. It constitutes *melachah*. Moses had a man stoned for gathering wood on the Sabbath; and the LORD commanded Israel not to go out of their places to gather manna on the Sabbath.[94]

THE THIRTY-NINE CATEGORIES

The judges over the nation of Israel had to make hard decisions about what constituted *melachah* and what did not. People's lives hung in the balance. Correctly understanding the legal definition of the word *melachah* could be a matter of life and death. The judges on a court of Torah could not convict or absolve people accused of Sabbath violations unless they had a standardized definition by which to make the judgment.

They determined any work that might have been performed as a part of the construction of the Tabernacle could be termed *melachah*. Employing this methodology, they derived thirty-nine specific categories (fathers) of *melachah*. Some of them arise directly from the biblical text, and most of them can be derived logically. The following translation of m.*Shabbat* 7:2 attempts to identify the internal logic in the list by inserting topic divisions.

"The principal fathers of *melachot* are forty lacking one:"

1. FROM FIELD TO LOAF — TOTALING ELEVEN ACTS

    Fieldwork—four acts

    "The one who plows, and the one who sows, and the one who reaps, and the one who binds sheaves ..."

    to Grain Processing—three acts

    "And the one who threshes, and the one who winnows, and the one who cleans [by sorting] ..."

    to Bread Production—four acts

    "And the one who grinds, and the one who sifts, and the one who kneads, and the one who bakes ..."

2. FROM SHEEP TO FABRIC — TOTALING THIRTEEN ACTS

    Wool Production—five acts

    "The one who shears the wool, and the one who bleaches [or washes] it, and the one who combs it, and the one who dyes it, and the one who spins it ..."

to Weaving—four acts

"And the one who stretches the warp, and the one who makes two loops [across the warp], and the one who weaves two threads, and the one who separates two threads ..."

to Finished Product—four acts

"The one who ties, and the one who unties, and the one who sews two stitches, and the one who tears out a portion to sew two stitches ..."

3. FROM HUNTING TO LEATHER PRODUCTION AND WRITING—TOTALING NINE ACTS

Securing the Hide—three acts

"The one who snares the deer, and the one who slaughters it, and the one who skins it ..."

to Producing Finished Leather—four acts

"And the one who salts it, and the one who prepares it, and the one who scrapes it, and the one who cuts it ..."

to Marking on Finished Parchment—two acts

"The one who writes two letters, and the one who erases a portion to write two letters ..."

4. VARIOUS ACTS OF PRODUCTION—TOTALING SIX ACTS

Building and Tearing Down—two acts

"The one who builds, and the one who tears down ..."

Fire for Blacksmithing—three acts

"The one who extinguishes, and the one who burns, and the one who hammers with a pattish ..."

Transporting—one act

"And the one who transports from one domain to another. Indeed, these are the forty principal fathers of *melachot* lacking one." (m.*Shabbat* 7:2)

The following overview of the thirty-nine "fathers" of labor provides a brief summary of the major concepts and their origin, but it should not be considered a comprehensive guide or halachic standard. Those seeking to learn how to keep the Sabbath by traditional Jewish standards should consult a halachic guide dedicated to that subject. Our purpose is only to demonstrate that, contrary to popular belief, the thirty-nine forms of prohibited labor are not merely rabbinic hot air. The sages derived them reasonably, and when the prohibited forms of labor are understood within their original agricultural context, they do not seem nearly as capricious or oppressive as they are commonly reputed to be. Even the derivative laws and stringencies have their own internal, logical consistency.

Jews who grew up in non-observant homes might feel overwhelmed by Sabbath halachah. From the outside, the details, stringencies, and enormous amount of technicalities look difficult and burdensome. On the contrary, the Jewish people have been observing the Sabbath by these standards for many long centuries. Children raised in observant homes do not feel oppressed by the weight of legislation; they delight in the Sabbath and anticipate its arrival all week long. Far from burdensome legalism, the Sabbath is a day of delight and holiness for the religious family.

Reading through the list of the thirty-nine *melachot* creates the false impression that the Sabbath must be enormously difficult to observe. Imagine if you had no previous experience driving a vehicle and had never seen one operated. You sit down to read a manual about how to drive an automobile. The numerous instructions are baffling. The choreography of litigious traffic rules seems baffling. On the other hand, when you watch a driver operate a vehicle and begin to learn to drive it yourself, you acquire the skills and necessary knowledge quickly and easily. The Sabbath is similar. It needs to be experienced, preferably with people already adept at observing it. Reading about it makes it sound complicated, confusing, and burdensome. Actually observing it, on the other hand, is a joy.

Christianity's negative assessment of the legislation defining the thirty-nine forms of labor is based on a misreading of the Sabbath-conflict stories in the gospels, which assumes that Jesus challenged the conventional Sabbath halachah. On the contrary, as we have seen, our Master accepted the halachah, but he argued that compassion for human beings should take priority over ceremonial prohibitions. He healed on the Sabbath because he prioritized alleviating human suffering above keeping the Sabbath.

Nevertheless, some will still complain that the Jewish observance of the Sabbath has been burdened with traditions of men and rules of rabbis. Before voicing those complaints, Gentile believers should keep in mind that neither the Torah nor the apostles nor even the rabbis require them to observe the Sabbath by abstaining from *melachah*. Therefore, the Gentile Sabbatarian need not feel threatened by the thirty-nine prohibitions whatsoever. Strictly speaking, they do not apply to him because a Gentile could not be convicted of violating the Sabbath by a court of law. The Gentile believer need not argue that the interpretation is wrong in order to justify his own preferences or to defend his own Sabbath practices.

The following chapter summarize the thirty-nine categories of *melachah* and some of the associated extensions.[95] Some believers, both Jews and Gentiles, will want to begin observing the Sabbath according to these standards. A believer should never be discouraged from better honoring the Sabbath, particularly Jewish believers who are actually not supposed to perform *melachah* on the Sabbath. At the same time, it may be best to take on higher levels of Sabbath observance slowly and methodically. A person can quickly become overwhelmed by the prohibitions. Keeping the Sabbath is never all or nothing, and something is always better than nothing. Moreover, a person should not look down on others who do not follow the traditional prohibitions. The Sabbath is poorly understood among Christians and Jewish believers. Anti-Sabbatarian teachings in the church have left many Jewish believers without any anchor in Sabbath observance. Moreover, the long years of exile have eroded Sabbath observance for most Jewish people, and no single individual can be held responsible for rectifying that.

CHAPTER THIRTEEN

From Field to Loaf

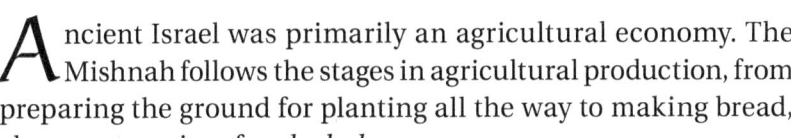

Ancient Israel was primarily an agricultural economy. The Mishnah follows the stages in agricultural production, from preparing the ground for planting all the way to making bread, eleven categories of *melachah*.

Plowing, planting, reaping, harvesting, threshing, and winnowing may not appear to be directly related to the construction of the Tabernacle, but they were in that the Tabernacle fabrics wove together linen (a fabric derived from flax), and the preparation of the Tabernacle required the loaves and bread offerings for the Tabernacle's inauguration.

1. PLOWING

The Torah specifically identifies plowing as a form of *melachah* when it says, "Six days you shall work, but on the seventh day you shall rest. In plowing time and in harvest you shall rest" (Exodus 34:21). Plowing (*choresh*, חורש) is clearly a form of *melachah*, but the traditional definition of plowing also includes any preparation or improvement of the ground such as smoothing, leveling, and raking. The prohibition includes digging in the garden, fertilizing, and working the soil in any manner.

2. SOWING

Planting and sowing (*zorea*, זורע) qualify as *melachah* because they are component of agriculture. They involves manipulating and taking mastery of nature. The prohibition not only forbids planting seeds, it includes any type of horticultural nurturing and care. Religious Jews will not even place cut flowers into water on the Sabbath day.

3. REAPING

Reaping and harvesting are also biblically identified as *melachah* and are included in the prohibition of Exodus 34:21: "In plowing time and in harvest you shall rest." Reaping (*kotzer*, קוצר) includes cutting, picking, or plucking any type of vegetation. Not only does this prohibit plucking an apple or picking a strawberry on the Sabbath, religious Jews will not pluck even a single blade of grass on the Sabbath day.

As we observed earlier, our Master's disciples did "what is not lawful to do on the Sabbath," i.e., "they began to pluck heads of grain and to eat" (Matthew 12:1–2). Yeshua defended his disciples on the basis of their extreme hunger according to his principle of prioritizing human need over ceremonial prohibitions, but he did not at all deny that by picking grain his disciples were violating the Sabbath. On the contrary, he argued that their extreme hunger made it permissible for them to violate the Sabbath.

ANIMALS

Animals cannot be used as pack animals or steeds on the Sabbath day, as it says, "that your ox and your donkey may rest" (Exodus 23:12). This prohibition also relates to the principle of not taking mastery over nature on the Sabbath day. Despite that, riding on a donkey does not really create anything. It is not formally a type of *melachah*, but the sages wanted to include the prohibition with the thirty-nine categories of forbidden labor. The prohibition on using animals is somewhat artificially connected to the prohibition on reaping: "There is a concern that one might forget and inadvertently pluck a branch for use as a switch."[96]

4. BINDING SHEAVES

The Mishnah's term "binding sheaves (*me'ammer*, מעמר)" refers to harvesting and gathering agricultural produce. The category includes other harvest procedures and preparations. For example, when harvesting olives, the harvester places sheets beneath the tree prior to beating the branches. A person might assume that, so long as he waited until after the Sabbath to beat the branches, he could place the sheets beneath the trees on the Sabbath. The broad prohibition on harvesting disallows it. Harvesting also includes gathering in general. For example, the Israelites were not allowed to gather manna on the Sabbath day, even though it did not need to be reaped.

5. THRESHING

Like plowing, planting, reaping, and harvesting, threshing is a form of agricultural production that constitutes *melachah*. Threshing (*dash*, דש) involves extracting grain from its husk, and by extension, it refers to all processes of extracting a usable substance from an unusable substance. Squeezing fruits to make fruit juice and crushing grapes and olives to extract their juice are included in this category. Nehemiah specifically mentions treading winepresses as a Sabbath violation.[97]

In Luke's version of the story of the grainfields, he mentions that the disciples husked the grain in their hands, an activity that constitutes a form of threshing: "His disciples plucked and ate some heads of grain, rubbing them in their hands" (Luke 6:1).

6. WINNOWING

Winnowing (*zoreh*, זורה) is a type of threshing and a form of agricultural mastery over nature. It involves separating grain from its chaff and husks by means of wind.

7. SORTING

The construction of the Tabernacle involved the *melachah* of selecting and sorting good materials from bad. The Mishnah refers to it as "sorting (*borer*, בורר)." Sorting consists of separating unwanted portions from wanted portions by hand. Originally, the prohibition on selecting had pertinence to agriculture. It prevented a farmer from separating bad produce from good produce on the Sabbath day. The prohibition on selecting can equally apply to other trades. For example, the Master tells a parable about fishermen, which involves sorting: "They sat down and sorted the good into containers but threw away the bad" (Matthew 13:48).

Rabbinic tradition extended the prohibition to food preparation and meals. A person eating from a bowl of cherries cannot pick out the bad ones first. (He may eat only the good ones though.) A person who uses a slotted spoon is sorting the solids and liquids in a soup. Similarly, this category forbids picking fish bones out of fish, which is why the boneless, ground *gefilte* fish is a favorite at the Sabbath table.

8. GRINDING

The construction of the Tabernacle involved various forms of grinding and milling (*tochen*, טוחן), whether with a millstone or with pestle and mortar. For example, the ingredients in the holy incense needed to be finely ground together. Like the above agricultural examples, grinding is also a type of agricultural production, which involves taking mastery over nature. The prohibition on grinding disallows the use of mills, grinders, mortars, and other forms of crushing.

The religious Jew does not crush garlic or grind spices on the Sabbath. The prohibition on grinding extends to prohibit grating things too, such as cheeses.

In the days of the apostles, medicines were prepared, as needed, by means of grinding. Therefore the sages forbade the use of non-vital medicines and medical treatments on the Sabbath day. This prohibition did not extend as far as life-threatening cases, but it may be the original source behind resistance to the Master's Sabbath-day healings.

9. SIFTING

The construction of the Tabernacle involved sifting (*merakked*, מרקד). This is a form of *melachah* that also relates to agricultural production. In biblical times, sifting was an important part of grain production: "As grain is shaken in a sieve, but not a kernel will fall to the ground" (Amos 9:9 NASB). Millers passed flour through sieves to separate the coarse from the fine. Tradition extends the prohibition on sifting into the kitchen by prohibiting the use of sieves, strainers, colanders, and other devices that might be used for sifting or straining during food preparation.

10. KNEADING

The construction of the Tabernacle involved kneading (*lash*, לש), which was a process of combining a powder substance with a liquid to make a paste or dough. This category includes making mud balls. When our Master spat on the ground, mixed his spittle with dirt, and applied the salve to the blind man's eyes, he violated the prohibition on kneading. Our Master's enemies declared, "This man is not from God, for he does not keep the Sabbath" (John 9:16).

11. COOKING (BOILING, BAKING, MELTING)

The construction of the Tabernacle entailed various forms of heating, boiling, baking, and melting—in other words, cooking with heat. The Torah explicitly identifies cooking food as a form of *melachah*. Exodus 16:23 prohibits cooking, baking, or boiling manna on the Sabbath, activities that the Mishnah refers to as "baking (*ofeh*, אופה)." This category includes boiling water and heating non-food items, even when the heating is accomplished without the use of flame. For example, baking in a microwave oven or a solar oven violates the Sabbath as much as using a conventional oven.

Does this mean that all Sabbath foods must be served cold? Not at all. Friday night meals are usually timed so that food for the Friday night Sabbath table is still hot. Precooked foods may be kept warm. For example, some homes place a tin sheet (called a *blech*) over the stovetop with the burners left on low to create a warm surface to maintain heat. The laws pertaining to keeping food warm are complex to explain but easy to carry out. The best way to learn how to manage a Shabbat kitchen is to learn from someone who is already familiar with the laws. Otherwise, a person should consult a guidebook that explains the rules.

The prohibition on cooking does not prevent other forms of food preparation such as cutting fruit, preparing a salad, and so forth. Furthermore, the prohibition on melting things does not extend so far as melting a pad of butter over warm food or using ice cubes to cool a drink.

Believers in Yeshua in ancient times kept the Sabbath prohibition on cooking. According to the long version of his epistle to the Magnesians, the early second-century Christian bishop Ignatius criticized other believers for keeping the Sabbath. He specifically mentioned food prepared in advance:

> Let every one of you keep the Sabbath after a spiritual manner ... not eating things prepared the day before, nor using lukewarm drinks, and walking within a prescribed space, nor finding delight in dancing and clapping which have no sense in them. (Ignatius, *Magnesians* 9:3, long version)

COOKING ON YOM TOV

In Jewish terminology, a festival on which work is restricted (that does not fall on the seventh day of the week) is referred to as a *Yom Tov*, that is, a "holiday." The Torah identifies seven such holidays: the first and seventh day of Pesach, the day of Shavu'ot, the day of Rosh Hashanah, the day of Yom Kippur, the first day of Sukkot, and the eighth day at the conclusion of Sukkot. The Torah forbids performing *melachah* on all the *Yamim Tovim*, but makes an exception for cooking (except for Yom Kippur on which no *melachah* may be performed whatsoever and a Yom Tov that falls on the weekly Sabbath).

Exodus 12:16 also identifies cooking as a form of *melachah* when it says, "No [*melachah*] shall be done on those days [i.e., the *Yom Tov* of Passover]. But what everyone needs to eat, that alone may be prepared by you" (Exodus 12:16). The exception clause in the passage makes it clear that food preparation is not allowed on the weekly Sabbath. Since Sabbath observance ordinarily prohibits that type of food preparation, the Torah had to expressly state that it is permitted on the *Yom Tov*; otherwise we would assume that it was prohibited as it is on the weekly Sabbath. The LORD permits food preparation on the *Yom Tov* to avoid hardship on Israel. A *Yom Tov* and the weekly Sabbath sometimes occur back-to-back. If the Torah prohibited food preparation on the *Yom Tov*, the prohibition would sometimes prevent a person from cooking or preparing food for more than forty-eight hours. Food cooked on *Yom Tov* must be cooked for consumption that same day (or on the ensuing day if it is also a sabbath). According to Jewish tradition, cooking fires can be ignited on *Yom Tov* only from a preexisting flame.

CHAPTER FOURTEEN
From Sheep to Fabric

The agriculture of ancient Israel involved wool production. The Mishnah follows the stages in fabric making, from sheep shearing to final product, identifying thirteen categories of *melachah*.

12. SHEARING

The construction of the Tabernacle required fabrics obtained from "shearing (*gozez*, גוזז) the wool" of sheep and goats. As an element of agricultural production and manufacturing, not to mention taking mastery over nature, shearing violates the Sabbath prohibition on *melachah*. Jewish interpretation includes shaving and haircuts. This includes all forms of removing hair or feathers from living creatures, including oneself. Religious Jews avoid even plucking eyebrows and using certain types of combs that might tear out hairs on the Sabbath.

13. WASHING

The construction of the Tabernacle required the preparation and washing of fabrics, specifically wool, a process the Mishnah refers to as "bleaching (*melabben*, מלבן)." Therefore, the sages categorize washing of fabrics as a form of *melachah*. This includes immersing and wringing fabrics and removing spots or stains. It does not prevent washing of dishes except that a dishcloth or sponge, since it is a fabric, should not be wrung out. Use of hot water is another issue that might fall under the prohibition on burning or cooking. Although it is not a form of *melachah,* Jewish tradition also prohibits bathing and showering on the Sabbath except under certain conditions.

14. COMBING

The construction of the Tabernacle required woolen threads. The process of rendering wool into fabric involves combing (*menappetz,* מנפץ) the wool, a form of *melachah* that prepares wool (and cotton) for use as thread. Obviously combing of wool or cotton is a component of production, manufacturing, and taking mastery over nature.

15. DYEING

The construction of the Tabernacle involved dyes to make "blue and purple and scarlet material," so the sages determined that the process of "dyeing (*tzovea,* צובע)" constitutes *melachah.* This includes all processes of changing something's color: dyeing, painting, adding a colored liquid to a clear liquid, mixing paints, and mixing cosmetics.

16. SPINNING

After the yarn-maker has thoroughly combed the wool, he may spin it into thread. The Mishnah refers to the process as "spinning (*toveh,* טווה)." The category of spinning includes associated forms of production such as making thread, rope, felt, and fabric: "And every skillful woman spun with her hands, and they all brought what they had spun in blue and purple and scarlet yarns and fine twined linen. All the women whose hearts stirred them to use their skill spun the goats' hair" (Exodus 35:25–26).

17. STRETCHING THE WARP

The construction of the Tabernacle involved setting up the warp of the loom in preparation for weaving. The Mishnah calls it "stretching (*meisech,* מיסך) the warp on the loom." Even though the warp without the weave was not a complete fabric, warping a loom is part of the process of *melachah* and therefore not permitted on the Sabbath.

18. MAKING TWO LOOPS

The construction of the Tabernacle involved the weaving process of setting up the woof of the loom. The Mishnah refers to it as "making two loops (*oseh shnei vatei nirin*, עושה שני בתי נירין)" the beginning of a woven web with two meshes, attaching them to the crosspieces or to the slips, i.e., preparing the loom to pass the spool with the woof across the warp. The broad application of the prohibition includes all types of needlecraft, knitting, crocheting, braiding, basketmaking, and net making.

19. WEAVING

The construction of the Tabernacle and the priestly garments required weaving, which the Torah explicitly identifies as *melachah*. The curtains, screens, and priestly vestments were the work of a weaver: "a weaver, as performers of every *melachah*" (Exodus 35:35). The Mishnah calls it "weaving (*oreg*, אורג) two threads." Weaving includes needlework like embroidery, needlepoint, basketmaking, and rug making. In legal terms, these restful, hobbies, activities, and handicrafts are no less violations of the Sabbath than carpentry and stonework.

20. SEPARATING TWO THREADS

If chainstitching, warping, and weaving are forms of *melachah*, the sages deemed that the opposite action of removing the woven product from the loom must be as well. The Mishnah refers to it as "separating (*potzea*, פוצע) two threads." It includes a general prohibition on unraveling fabrics.

21. TYING

The construction of the Tabernacle involved tying knots to fasten together fabrics and curtains and fasten tent cords. The sages inferred that some forms of tying knots can constitute *melachah*. The Mishnah refers to "tying (*kosher*, קושר)" any type of permanent knot, such as a sail knot, as *melachah*. The prohibition does not apply to temporary knots, such tying one's shoes or necktie.

22. UNTYING

If knotting was part of the construction of the Tabernacle and a form of *melachah*, then the inverse is also. The Mishnah calls it "untying (*mattir*, מתיר)." Jewish tradition permits the untying of temporary knots, such as one's shoes or necktie, but knots intended as permanent knots should not be untied on the Sabbath.

The sages, however, specifically permitted the tying and untying of knots for the purpose of leashing animals and drawing water.[98] Yeshua took it for granted that tying and untying knots violates the Sabbath. He also took it for granted than an exception must be made for the sake of watering one's animal:

> Does not each of you on the Sabbath untie his ox or his donkey from the manger and lead it away to water it? And ought not this woman, a daughter of Abraham whom Satan bound for eighteen years, be loosed from this bond on the Sabbath day? (Luke 13:15–16)

23. SEWING

The construction of the Tabernacle involved stitching and sewing fabrics, an activity the Mishnah calls "sewing (*tofer*, תופר) two stitches." Sewing certainly constitutes *melachah*. The prohibition on sewing includes all forms of stitchery, needlework, knitting, etc. Jewish law includes pasting, gluing, taping, and stapling under the same category. Applying adhesive stamps, stickers, or sealing an envelope are also forms of *melachah* under the same category. The rule does permit fastening objects with temporary fasteners, such as a safety pin.

24. TEARING

The construction of the Tabernacle involved tearing, a category of *melachah* that includes rending fabrics. The Mishnah calls it "tearing (*korea,* קורע) in order to sew two stitches." By extension, the law prohibits separating glued papers or other objects affixed by adhesives or permanent fastenings. For example, opening the lid on a box of cereal involves separating the adhesive and is not permitted.

CHAPTER FIFTEEN

From Hunting to Leather Production and Writing

The exterior of the Tabernacle was protected by a covering of tanned skins. Several classes of labor relate to the process of preparing hides, beginning with hunting or trapping an animal. Ancient Israel depended on the tanning industry for the production of leather and parchments. The Mishnah follows the stages in tanning, parchment making, to writing, identifying nine categories of *melachah*.

25. TRAPPING

The Mishnah refers to trapping an animal as "snaring (*tzad*, צד) a deer." Trapping an animal takes mastery over nature. The sages regard setting traps, hunting, and capturing wild animals as a form of *melachah*. This stands to reason. If gathering manna was forbidden on the Sabbath, how much more so is the pursuit of wild game contrary to the Sabbath. This category includes fishing. However, one may trap a dangerous animal in order to protect people from harm.

Sportsmen might protest that hunting and fishing are legitimate Sabbath activities because they are a means of relaxation and a way to enjoy the outdoors, but many prohibited forms of labor are also sources of relaxation and enjoyment. Pursuing, trapping, hunting, and gathering game certainly violates the Sabbath. Sportsmen should consider who it is that provides fish for their hooks and game for their gunsights. Will he not bless the sportsman who honors his Sabbath?

26. SLAUGHTERING

The construction of the Tabernacle required the slaughter of animals to procure their hides for the covering of the tent of meeting. The Mishnah considers "slaughtering (*shochet*, שוחט) an animal" to be a form of *melachah*. Religious Jews try to avoid all types of slaughtering on the Sabbath, even to the point of sparing the lives of insects on the holy day. The prohibition extends to all forms of killing or injuring. The Sabbath is a day for life, not death. Killing imposes the killer's will and takes mastery over nature. Of course, one may kill to save a life or protect people from harm. The sacrificial services in the Temple create another important exception to the rule. The priests in the Temple have a commandment to carry out the Sabbath-day sacrifices. Yeshua observed that, according to the Torah, the priests in the temple broke the Sabbath to carry out the sacred service, yet they were guiltless.[99]

27. SKINNING

Procuring skins for the Tabernacle involved flaying and skinning animals. The Mishnah refers to this form of *melachah* as "skinning (*mafshit*, מפשיט)," the first step in the tanning process. This prohibition includes all forms of gutting animals, such as cleaning fish, and it includes processing meat.

28. TANNING

Tanning is a process by which hides are made into leather. The Mishnah refers to it as "salting (*moleach*, מולח)" and "preparing (*me'abbed*, מעבד) a hide," the early stages in the tanning process. Tanners also rub oil and saddle soap into the hides.

29. SCRAPING

The tanning process involves scraping the hair from the hides and smoothing the surface of the skin. The Mishnah refers to it as "scraping (*memachek*, ממחק)." The category includes all smoothing and polishing operations. Religious Jews do not polish shoes, silver, or even the lenses of eyeglasses on the Sabbath day.

On that basis, Jewish interpretation bans the application of lotions, salves, and medications which must be smeared onto the skin, such as lipstick. Our Master smeared mud and spittle onto the blind man's eyes to demonstrate that the alleviation of human suffering takes priority over the Sabbath.

30. CUTTING

The construction of the Tabernacle involved cutting objects. The Mishnah calls it "cutting (*mechattech*, מחתך)." The prohibition on cutting applies to changing the size or shape of an object to make it more useful, such as chopping a piece of wood or tearing a piece of paper into a certain shape, hence the proverbial pre-torn toilet paper. Foods for the Sabbath day, however, are exempt from the prohibition since they are not permanent and will be shortly consumed. The category of cutting also includes shaping and forming. It takes no great leap of logic to see that shaping and reshaping are a type of *melachah*. The *melachah* of creation from which God rested on the seventh day includes the act of shaping. He shaped the first man from the clay. Obviously, acts of shaping like spinning pots on a wheel or carving wood are forms of prohibited work. Unfortunately, shaping includes making snowmen. Even snowballs are problematic, not so much because they involve shaping, but because they involve crushing and compacting in order to create.

31. WRITING

The construction of the Tabernacle required marking and writing. A person might not think of writing notes as a form of *melachah*, but writing something down on paper or on any other type of permanent medium creates a document. The Mishnah refers to it as "writing (*kotev*, כותב) two letters." The prohibition on writing includes handwriting, typing, printing, photocopying, stamping, and record-keeping. Drawing, sketching, etching, scribbling, doodling, highlighting, and underlining all fall into the same category. A rabbinic stringency forbids games of chance since they ordinarily involve notations and record keeping. *Pictionary* and tic-tac-toe are definitely off-limits.

The prohibition on writing also precludes all activities that require the creation of a written document such as conducting a marriage (which requires the signing of a *ketubbah*), issuing a divorce (which requires writing a divorce certificate), and business arrangements (which require creating and signing contracts).

32. ERASING

The construction of the Tabernacle may or may not have involved erasing, but if writing is a form of *melachah*, it stands to reason that the inverse is also. The Mishnah refers to it as "erasing (*mochek*, מוחק) a portion to write two letters."

The Mishnah was only concerned with erasing for the purpose of rewriting, but rabbinic stringencies extended the prohibition to forbid any form of destroying written letters on the Sabbath. That means no erasing letters, tearing through letters, smudging out letters, or any other form of deleting text. Chalkboards and dry erase boards are not Sabbath-friendly.

CHAPTER SIXTEEN

Various Acts of Production

The remaining six categories of *melachah* are a miscellaneous assortment of prohibited forms of work. The Mishnah derived some, such as igniting a fire and carrying a load, directly from the biblical text, and others are logically inferred from the construction of the Tabernacle.

33. BUILDING

The construction of the Tabernacle involved "building (*boneh*, בונה)." This broad category includes all types of construction and repair. Jewish law includes pitching a tent as a form of building, and rabbinic opinions extend that to even small acts such as opening an umbrella (which is the same as pitching a very small tent). The general category of building includes all types of assembly projects. Sabbath is not the day for building an addition on your house, tearing down an old wall, or even for assembling a doghouse. Nails, hammers, pry-bars, and other tools have nothing to contribute to the Sabbath. Even the holy Tabernacle was not to be built on the Sabbath day, how much less the mundane projects which we deem so important.

34. DEMOLISHING

The opposite of assembling is disassembly, and the Mishnah refers to it as "demolishing (*soter*, סותר)." On the level of biblical concern, demolishing involves only destroying in order to build, such as removing broken parts for replacement or tearing down a wall to replace it later. It includes all forms of dismantling anything that cannot be built on the Sabbath. Even taking down a tent on the Sabbath is a form of *melachah*. On the other hand, tearing down a tower of toy blocks is permitted, because building a tower of toy blocks is permitted.

35. EXTINGUISHING

The building of the Tabernacle required various forms of extinguishing flame. For example, a fire used to heat a material must be extinguished to prevent the metal from overheating. According to one opinion, the prohibition pertains to extinguishing a fire to produce charcoal.

The sages reasoned that if igniting and feeding a fire constitutes *melachah* (see below), it makes sense that extinguishing a fire does so as well. The Mishnah refers to it as "extinguishing flame (*mechabbeh*, מכבה)." This interpretation does not arise directly from the biblical text. The reasoning is not clear, but it seems to be in keeping with the idea of taking mastery over nature and imposing our will onto something. Extinguishing fire is as much a part of the production process as igniting fire. For example, a man who makes maple syrup might say, "It is not permissible to make a fire on Sabbath, therefore I will make the fire before Sabbath begins. Then I need only put out the fire when the syrup has been rendered."

In Jewish homes, Sabbath candles are left to burn down; thermostats and stoves are not adjusted. Lights are not turned off. As always, the Sabbath must be violated when necessary to save life. Thus the traditional halachah requires one to put out a fire if it constitutes a threat to life.

36. BURNING FIRE

The building of the Tabernacle required burning fires for a variety of stages in production. Fire, a key component in smithing, is a basic rudiment in manufacturing and one of the primary means by which man takes mastery over nature to alter it in some fashion.

The Torah defines making a fire as *melachah*. It explicitly states: "You shall kindle no fire in any of your dwelling places on the Sabbath day" (Exodus 35:3). Making a fire (*mav'ir*, מבעיר) includes both igniting and feeding a fire.

This law explains why we light candles before the Sabbath begins. The Sabbath candles are a remembrance of the days when candles and lamps provided the only source of illumination. If a person wanted light on the Sabbath, he had to insure that the lamps were lit before the Sabbath began.

Non-Jewish readers sometimes argue that the Torah only prohibited making a fire on the Sabbath because making a fire was a lot of work in those days. One needed kindling, wood, and a flame source. In modern times, simply turning on the stove or flicking a cigarette lighter produces effortless flame—it does not take much work at all. This is faulty thinking. The Torah does not prohibit making a fire on the Sabbath day because it required a lot of work. It did not. The ancient Israelites were not cavemen rubbing sticks together. The amount of effort involved in the process has no relevance. The Torah simply says not to "burn a fire" with no indication of whether it was easily lit or not.

Burning something constitutes a form of *melachah* because it involves intentionally transforming one substance into another. When we burn something, whether it is a log in the fire or the butane in a cigarette lighter, we engage in a process of manipulating the elements of the creation (oxidation) to pass from matter (solid or gas) to energy. We are shaping, forming, making, and creating. *Melachah* means making things, and fire makes heat, light, smoke, and ash.

The prohibition on burning means that things like smoking a cigarette or pipe are forbidden on the Sabbath. A gasoline engine burns gasoline; therefore, one cannot drive a car on the Sabbath. (Electric cars are a different matter. See below.) Observant Jews take note of even less-obvious forms of burning. For example, drawing hot water from a gas-burning water heater causes the water heater to burn more gas to heat the water.

How do Sabbath keepers survive in cold climates? Would not a Sabbath-keeping family freeze to death? Saving life always takes precedence over the Sabbath. In a desperate situation, the Sabbath keeper would light a fire. In most cases, such emergency measures would be unnecessary. Stoves can be heated in advance, set up with fuel-feeders, and heat can be stored in water and stone. Even more useful, friendly Gentile neighbors can help by firing up stoves on cold mornings because the Torah does not prohibit non-Jews from voluntarily performing *melachah* on the Sabbath (even though it does prohibit non-Jews from doing so as the servant or agent of a Jew).

ELECTRICITY AND BURNING

According to some opinions, heating a metal filament to the point at which it glows is also a form of burning; therefore, flipping a light switch to turn on the lights violates the Sabbath. According to many opinions, electricity has the same halachic status as fire.[100] The Torah sometimes refers to lightning as "fire." Observant Jews do not turn appliances or electrical devices off or on during the Sabbath, nor do they operate any devices that use electricity.

Some opinions prohibit the use of electricity on other grounds, such as the idea that completing a circuit constitutes "finishing." For example, electricity is a type of wave and particle like light itself, and the Bible specifically categorizes the creation of light as a form of *melachah* in the creation narrative.

Imagine a world without smartphones, handheld tablets and pads, computers, music players, electronic games, and other electronic devices. That world is called the Sabbath. All traditional opinions agree that using electrical devices at least violates the spirit of the Sabbath. Lights turned on before the Sabbath are left on. Telephones and mobile devices are used only in a life-and-death emergency.

37. FINISHING

The construction of the Tabernacle entailed a variety of tasks categorized as "finishing" or "completing." The Mishnah refers to it as "striking with a hammer (*makkeh bepattish*, מכה בפטיש)," an idiom for completing a job. The biblical text does not specifically prohibit this general category, but it certainly implies it in the creation narrative: "God *finished* his work that he had done, and he rested on the seventh day from all his work that he had done" (Genesis 2:2).

The general category of "finishing" includes all forms of repairs or completions of projects. Examples include sanding, planing, carving, painting, shaping, sharpening, and assembling. Any finishing touch on a project falls under this category.

Traditional interpretation includes adjustments to mechanical devices such as winding a clock, setting a watch, or tuning a musical instrument. The rabbis forbade the use of all musical instruments on the Sabbath lest the musician feel compelled to tune the instrument. (Levitical musicians were permitted to use instruments on the Sabbath in the Temple, much as the priests were permitted to carry out their Temple duties on the Sabbath.)

The prohibition on finishing prevents making an unusable object usable on the Sabbath. Light repairs, like changing a bulb, fall under this prohibition. Finishing includes reaffixing a bicycle chain, and for that reason, religious Jews do not ride bicycles on the Sabbath. Even something as mundane as threading new laces into a pair of shoes can be considered finishing.

SAILING AND SWIMMING

The construction of the Tabernacle involved neither sailing nor swimming, but the rabbis considered making adjustments to a sail in order to catch the wind to be a type of finishing, therefore they banned sailing on the Sabbath. Harnessing the wind involves taking mastery over nature. Jewish law allows a Jewish person to ride as a passenger on a sailing vessel operated by a non-Jew on the Sabbath, so long as the Sabbath keeper does not embark or disembark on the Sabbath day. Although swimming has nothing to do with finishing or any of the other categories of *melachah*, a special rabbinic enactment forbids swimming on the Sabbath. Religious Jews do not go to the beach on Saturday afternoons.

38. CARRYING

The building of the Tabernacle required carrying objects from one place to another. Carrying a load constitutes *melachah* and is forbidden on the Sabbath. The Mishnah refers to it as "transferring an object from one domain to another (*hamotzi mereshut lirshut*, המוציא מרשות לרשות)." Contrary to popular belief, the prohibition on carrying a load is not a rabbinic innovation. This is one of the few categories specifically mentioned in the Bible. Rabbinic legislation is responsible for the interpretation of the prohibition and further extensions on the interpretation, but the law against carrying arises indirectly from the Torah (Exodus 16:29; Numbers 15:32–36) and directly from the prophet Jeremiah:

> Take care for the sake of your lives, and do not bear a burden on the Sabbath day or bring it in by the gates of Jerusalem. And do not carry a burden out of your houses on the Sabbath or do any work, but keep the Sabbath day holy, as I commanded your fathers. (Jeremiah 17:21–22)

A person might argue that the "burden" or "load" referred to in Jeremiah 17 must be a load of merchandise. That may be the case, but traditional Jewish interpretation has defined the load more broadly to include moving any object carried from a private domain into a public domain and any object carried in a public domain four cubits or more. Jewish law extends that definition even to trivial objects like a house key or gloves in the pockets.

In any case, the prohibition on carrying a load only applies outside of one's home. Carrying within one's home or within a private domain is permissible. The Bible says, "Do not carry a burden out of your houses on the Sabbath day," but it does not prohibit carrying a load within one's home.

The terms "public domain" and "private domain" used in Jewish law can be somewhat misleading, because they do not refer to whether a space is publically or privately owned. A public domain is a large, open space with a substantial amount of traffic, such as the main thoroughfare of a town. A private domain is an area that is enclosed by walls or certain kinds of natural borders.

Some places are neither completely private property nor completely public, such as a courtyard shared with a neighboring house. Jewish law determines that carrying in this type of area is not technically prohibited on a biblical level. However, since it is not always easy to tell whether or not an area is truly "public," it is forbidden to carry in this semi-public area only as a rabbinic safeguard. In those situations, a carefully defined border can be used to include the semi-public domain within the private domain, thereby allowing carrying within the combined space (*eruv*). The Talmud discusses these complicated laws in tractates *Eruvin* and *Shabbat*, but, in general, it means that an adjacent area can be declared to be part of one's private home.

Disciples of Yeshua remember that the Master told a crippled man to "pick up his mat and carry it" on the Sabbath day. Does this mean that Yeshua disregarded the Sabbath or that he made the law forbidding carrying a load obsolete? On the contrary, as we have seen, he taught that compassion for human suffering and the dignity of his fellow Jew should take priority over the uncertainties of carrying or not carrying in a semi-public domain.

CARRYING A LOAD = BUYING AND SELLING

Carrying is allowed within one's home, but Jewish tradition also forbids even handling things which may not be used on the Sabbath, such as tools, pencils, candles, money, wallets, weapons, etc. This rabbinic safeguard can be compared with telling your children, "Don't play with matches."

The prohibition on carrying a load also forbids all types of financial transactions on the Sabbath day, transfer of property, transfer of ownership, buying, selling, trading, and commerce. These extensions are not rabbinic stringencies, they are explicit in the Bible.[101] Sabbath-observant people do not use money, neither cash nor credit, on the Sabbath day. Religious Jews will not even handle money on the Sabbath. All business transactions stop, including electronic purchases and exchanges. Perhaps Paul instructed the Corinthian believers to set aside a portion of their money on the first day of the week because of the taboo around handling money and finances on the Sabbath.[102]

Money represents work. Every society uses currency as a token of a person's labor, effort, and time. If a person works for a wage of $10 an hour, then a $5 bill represents one-half hour of work.

The prohibition on financial transactions also includes hiring services on the Sabbath. Going to a restaurant entails paying for the hire of someone else's *melachah* and the purchase of food. Nehemiah saw buying and selling, even the buying and selling of food, as an "evil thing" and a "profaning" of the Sabbath. According to Nehemiah, buying and selling constitute as much a desecration of the Sabbath as treading winepresses or loading donkeys.[103]

39. MARKING

The construction of the Tabernacle required various forms of marking and scoring. The sages designated marking and cutting the hides of animals as a category of *melachah*: marking out lines or scoring surfaces in preparation for cutting or working on a piece. Hence one should not take measurements and make markings on the Sabbath day, even if the actual cutting or fitting is not done on the Sabbath. Marking and measuring in anticipation of a project violates the spirit of the Sabbath.

Note that the Mishnah does not list "marking" as one of the thirty-nine forms of *melachah*. Instead, the Mishnah seems to list "salting" and "preparing" as two separate things, but the Gemara objects that they are both the same. That left the sages with only thirty-eight. They added marking (*mesartet*, משרטט) to fill out the number.[104]

CONCLUSION

Judge with Right Judgment

CONCLUSION

Judge with Right Judgment

JOHN 7:24

When viewed as Jewish literature, the Gospel stories about Jesus' conflicts with the sages of his day look like typical halachic disputations, such as the type that pepper the volumes of the Mishnah and Talmud. His arguments about whether or not healing and acts of compassion override the Sabbath are the same type of argumentation in which the sages and rabbis routinely engaged. They did so to keep the sacred charge Moses issued to the judges and legislators: "Judge the people with righteous judgment" (Deuteronomy 16:18). The Great Assembly of Ezra's generation reiterated the charge: "Be deliberate in judgment."[105] In the Gospel of John, Jesus reminded his colleagues of that responsibility when he concluded his halachic argument for healing on the Sabbath. With a clear reference to Deuteronomy 16:18, he said, "Do not judge by appearances, but judge with right judgment" (John 7:24).

The same admonition applies to us.

Traditional Christian interpretation has judged by mere appearances. From a simple, cursory reading of the Gospels, it does *appear* that Jesus must have been a Sabbath breaker. His disciples broke the Sabbath when they plucked grain on the Sabbath; he defended them. That makes him *appear* to have no regard for the sanctity of the Sabbath.

He broke the Sabbath by healing people on the Sabbath. He healed a man with a withered arm on the Sabbath; he healed a man with dropsy right at the Sabbath table of prominent sages; he healed a woman with a bent back, straightening the bent, on the Sabbath. All of these are obvious violations of the Sabbath. These stories make him *appear* to disregard God's laws against performing acts of work (*melachah*) on the Sabbath.

He told a man to carry his mat home on the Sabbath. This makes it *appear* that he disagreed with the traditional laws of honoring the Sabbath by not carrying objects outside a private domain.

Judging by *mere appearances,* it looks like Jesus was all about abolishing the Sabbath. Traditional Christian interpretation assumes that the Master did these things to send an implicit message that the Sabbath is no longer binding. We have failed to judge with right judgment.

Likewise, anti-missionaries in the Jewish community judge by mere appearances. They point out, somewhat gleefully, that Jesus cannot be the Messiah of Israel, nor can he be considered a sinless righteous man, because he flagrantly broke the Sabbath and taught others to do so as well. These critics of our Master make the same allegations against him that his enemies among the religious leaders made two thousand years ago. Ironically, we, his disciples, have affirmed those allegations because we too have judged his teachings about the Sabbath by mere appearances.

As we have seen, even Christian Sabbatarians and Messianic believers who reject the notion that Jesus abrogated the Sabbath usually interpret these incidents to mean that Jesus did not accept the particulars of Sabbath law. It is popular to explain that he broke the "rabbinic" and "man-made" traditions about Sabbath in order to show everyone that Jewish interpretation of the law is illegitimate. Therefore, he let his disciples husk grain on the Sabbath; he healed on the Sabbath; and he made mud on the Sabbath to demonstrate that the thirty-nine types of labor (*melachah*) prohibited by Jewish law on the Sabbath may be safely disregarded. Again, we have judged by mere appearances and failed to judge with right judgment.

If picking and husking grain, healing a withered arm, lifting an ox out of a pit, and tethering and un-tethering an ox or donkey to lead it to water, mixing mud and spittle, applying salve, and carrying a mat did not actually constitute legal violations of Shabbat, Jesus would have simply said so. He would not have bothered with halachic justifications which attempted to demonstrate why such acts should be permissible under certain circumstances. For example, if he believed healing on the Sabbath was not an actual violation of the Sabbath, he would not have compared healing with circumcision.

Jesus taught that, at times and under certain compelling circumstances, a man must break the Sabbath in order to keep another, weightier commandment. This halachic (legal) principle connects and unites all of the Gospel's Sabbath stories. It reveals a legal consistency that, rather than abrogating traditional Jewish Sabbath legislation, actually upholds a halachic approach to Sabbath and Jewish law.

If we judge Jesus with right judgment, the evidence compels us to admit that he upheld the Sabbath and practiced it according to the norms of Jewish practice in his day. Only when a weightier matter arose, such as demonstrating *chesed* for another human being, did he feel justified in setting aside the prohibitions of the holy day—be they biblical or traditional prohibitions.

By logical extension, the same principle may be applied to other ceremonial concerns. Compassion for one's fellow human being takes priority. Alleviating human suffering should be sufficient cause to set aside ceremonial functions. This principle illustrates our Master's greatest teachings about the precedence of love.

> For the commandments, "You shall not commit adultery, You shall not murder, You shall not steal, You shall not covet," and any other commandment, are summed up in this word: "You shall love your neighbor as yourself." Love does no wrong to a neighbor; therefore love is the fulfilling of the [Torah]. (Romans 13:9–10)

Endnotes

1. E.g., Deuteronomy 13:1–5, 17:15–20. Cf. Ezekiel 37:24–25.
2. Several manuscripts of Luke 6:1 specify the Sabbath with the strange word *deuteroprotos* (δευτερόπρωτος) which means "second of the first." The KJV renders, "And it came to pass on the second sabbath after the first ..." The Young's Literal Translation has, "And it came to pass, on the second-first sabbath." The DHE translates Luke 6:1 to say, "On the second *Shabbat* day of the counting of the *omer* he was passing among the fields." Delitzsch took some liberty with the Greek to arrive at that translation. The Torah commands the Jewish people to count a series of seven weeks (literally seven Sabbaths) between the feasts of Passover and Pentecost—an interval of forty-nine days called "the counting of the [barley] omer" (see Leviticus 23:9–16). Several scholars agree that the "Second-first Sabbath" of Luke 6:1 must refer to the second Sabbath during that forty-nine day interval. Marshall (*The Gospel of Luke* [New International Greek Testament Commentary; Grand Rapids, MI: Eerdmans Publishing, 1978], 230) explains it as "the second Sabbath after the feast of Unleavened Bread (Nisan 15), the first Sabbath being that which fell during the actual week of the feast; this would give a date between Nisan 22 and 30." See also Shmuel Safrai, "Sabbath Breakers," *Jerusalem Perspective* 3:4 (July/August 1990): 3–5.
3. Safrai, "The Sabbath Breakers"; m.*Bava Metzia* 7:2–5.
4. Leviticus 19:9–10, 23:22; Deuteronomy 24:19–21. Did the disciples qualify as "the poor" who were eligible for gleaning and taking from the corners of the field? They may have, but their poverty was voluntary. After the gleaners have already gone over a field, the remaining gleanings were considered to be fair game for anyone. Safrai ("The Sabbath Breakers") explains, "The halachah allowed a person to enter a field after the harvest had been completed and after the poor had collected the gleanings allotted them by the Torah:

'When is everyone permitted to collect gleanings? When the last of the poor have left' (Mishnah, *Peah* 8:1)."

5   The thirty-nine *melachot* (מלאכות). m.*Shabbat* 7:2. David Instone-Brewer dates these back to the days of the Master. See David Instone-Brewer, *Traditions of the Rabbis from the Era of the New Testament, Volume 2a: Feasts and Sabbaths—Passover and Atonement* (Grand Rapids, MI: Eerdmans, forthcoming), 32–36.

6   Exodus 34:21, 35:3; Numbers 15:32–36; Jeremiah 17:21–22. For a full list of prohibited Shabbat activities that are explicitly mentioned in the biblical text, see Nahum Sarna, *The JPS Torah Commentary: Exodus* (New York: The Jewish Publication Society, 1991), 112.

7   Shlomo Pines (*The Jewish Christians of the Early Centuries of Christianity According to a New Source* [Jerusalem: Central Press, 1966], 63) has found manuscript evidence from what he believes to be remnants of ancient Jewish Christian texts that record the disciples rubbed and ate the grain heads but did not pluck them. This he states would have been permissible according to Rabbi Judah's opinion in b.*Shabbat* 128a, provided that it was done within Sabbath limits. This explanation, however, contradicts the narrative of the Gospels where the Pharisees clearly understand the action of the disciples to be in violation of the Sabbath. It also requires an emendation of all three synoptic accounts, removing the language about the disciples picking grain. Safrai ("Sabbath Breakers," 3–5) and Flusser (*The Sage from Galilee: Rediscovering Jesus' Genius* [Grand Rapids, MI: Eerdmans, 2007], 34–35) advance the same opinion and cite Pines. All three scholars share common ground in that all three were observant Jews who understood that Yeshua could not have arbitrarily declared the Sabbath laws irrelevant to his disciples. Yet their proposed solution is inadequate because it requires textual emendations, and it leaves the ensuing halachic exchange with the Pharisees incomprehensible.

8   Herbert W. Basser, *Studies in Exegesis: Christian Critiques of Jewish Law and the Rabbinic Responses 70–300 CE* (Boston, MA: Brill Academic Publishers, 2002), 20. Hereafter referred to as Basser, *Studies in Exegesis*.

9   Yechiel Tzvi Lichtenstein, (*Commentary on the New Testament: The Holy Gospel According to Mark* ([Unpublished, Marshfield, MO: Vine of David, 2010], on Mark 3:4; originally published in Hebrew: *Beiur LeSiphrei Brit HaChadashah,* [Leipzig: Professor G. Dahlman, 1897]) comes close to this interpretation as he explains that the prohibition on healing on the Sabbath is only a rabbinic interpretation (*de-rabbanan*), a decree to prevent one from grinding herbs, and not the literal intention of the Torah, and therefore Yeshua felt free to transgress it but would never have transgressed the literal commandment. Lichtenstein is right about the *de-rabbanan*

interpretation of the ban on healing, but he is mistaken when he supposes that the Master justified setting aside a *de-rabbanan* ruling but not a literal commandment.

10   According to Basser (*Studies in Exegesis*, 27), the type of harvesting the disciples engaged in might have been permissible by some opinions since they harvested in an unusual manner—by hand and not with a sickle—but the sages extended this through the principle *shanui* (change from a regular manner, שנוי) and would have prohibited this type of harvesting rabbinically. In any case, Yeshua did not argue with the Pharisees on the basis of how the harvesting was performed. Instead, he accepted that the disciples were in violation of Sabbath law, and he defended them from that perspective.

11   1 Samuel 21:2–7(1–6). The text of Mark introduces a problem. Mark 2:26 misidentifies the priest on duty at Nob as Abiathar and even calls him the high priest: "He entered the house of God in the time of Abiathar *the* high priest, and ate the consecrated bread." Abiathar was the son of Ahimelech, the only survivor of Saul's slaughter of the priests at Nob. The name Abiathar is omitted from the story in both Matthew and Luke. Anti-missionaries and critics of the gospel point this out as a gaff on Yeshua's part. Lichtenstein (*Commentary on the New Testament*, on Mark 2:26) responds, "It seems to me that what Yeshua meant was that Abiathar became high priest immediately following the death of Ahimelech, at the hand of Saul, and that at the time David was with Ahimelech and took the bread [of the Presence], Abiathar was with him and did not protest to his father about this, and perhaps even assisted his father in this matter." Lichtenstein goes on to note that even the Tanach has some confusion between the names Ahimelech and Abiathar. Abiathar generally appears as David's priest serving along with Zadok, but 2 Samuel 8:17 and 1 Chronicles 24:6 name him "Ahimelech son of Abiathar." As R.T. France (*The Gospel of Mark* [New International Greek Testament Commentary; Grand Rapids, MI: Eerdmans Publishing, 2002], 146) puts it, "Mark seems to share the confusion."

12   Leviticus 24:9.

13   See Brad Young, *Jesus the Jewish Theologian* (Peabody, MA: Hendrickson, 1996), 107.

14   1 Samuel 21:6. Cf. Leviticus 24:8.

15   The Master employed the rabbinic principle of *tsad heter* (צד התר), where a precedent is cited to show that in a certain circumstance a law can be relaxed. Basser, *Studies in Exegesis*, 28, n. 39.

16   E.g., Leviticus 24:6–8; Numbers 28:9–10, etc.; Yechiel Tzvi Lichtenstein (*Commentary on the New Testament: The Holy Gospel According to Mattai* [Unpublished, Marshfield, MO: Vine of David, 2010], on

Matthew 12:5; originally published in Hebrew: *Beiur LeSiphrei Brit HaChadashah*, [Leipzig: Professor G. Dahlman, 1897]) cites m.*Pesachim* 6:1 as an example: "These are matters related to the Passover offering that override *Shabbat*: slaughtering it, sprinkling its blood, removal of waste from its internal organs, and burning its fat portions. But roasting it, and rinsing its internal organs do not override *Shabbat*. Transporting it, bringing it outside the border of permitted *Shabbat* travel, and the cutting of its warts do not override *Shabbat*. Rabbi Eli'ezer says: They do override it." Strangely, both Mark and Luke omit Yeshua's second example about the priesthood on the Sabbath day from their narrative. Matthew preserves the full version of the Master's argument.

17   *Mekilta* on Exodus 31:12.
18   b.*Yoma* 85b.
19   R. Steven Notley, "Greater Than the Temple," n.p. [Cited 27 April 2010]. Online: http://www.jerusalemperspective.com/Default.aspx?tabid=27&ArticleID=1757.
20   b.*Berachot* 31b.
21   The Master's introductory phrase, "If you had known what this means," is similar in style to formulas found for citing Scripture in rabbinic arguments. Krister Stendahl, *The School of St. Matthew and Its Use of the Old Testament* (Ramsey, NJ: Sigler Press, 1991), 128–129.
22   Lichtenstein, *Commentary on the New Testament*, on Matthew 12:7.
23   b.*Yoma* 85b; *Mekilta* on Exodus 31:14.
24   Cf. Young, *Jesus the Jewish Theologian*, 109–110.
25   E.g., b.*Shabbat* 119a.
26   Alternatively, as Delitszch renders it, *"Adon HaShabbat* (אדון השבת)," but *Adon* can also be used to mean "husband."
27   Mark 2:28; Matthew 12:8; Luke 6:5.
28   See Geza Vermes, "The Use of בר נש/בר נשא in Jewish Aramaic," in Matthew Black, *An Aramaic Approach to the Gospels and Acts* (Oxford: Clarendon Press, 1967), 310–330.
29   E.g., Enoch 46:1–3, 62:4–6.
30   See Young, *Jesus the Jewish Theologian*, 111; Samuel Tobias Lachs, *A Rabbinic Commentary on the New Testament: The Gospels of Matthew, Mark and Luke* (Hoboken, NJ: KTAV Publishing House, 1987), 198; Notley, "Sabbath Was Made for Man," n.p.
31   When the Hebrew equivalent to the Greek text is *ba'al HaShabbat* (בעל השבת).
32   Lichtenstein, *Commentary on the New Testament*, on Matthew 12:8.
33   Marshall, *The Gospel of Luke*, 233.

34 Rabbi Lichtenstein refers to the Sabbath Agraphon as "an absolute lie" fabricated by Greeks who hated the Torah of Moses. Lichtenstein, *Commentary on the New Testament*, on Matthew 12:8. His strong words were a reaction to Christian missionaries who had translated the agraphon into Hebrew to encourage Jewish Christians to abandon the Sabbath. But see Joachim Jeremias (*Unknown Sayings of Jesus*, [New York: Macmillan Company, 1957], 49–54) defends the authenticity of the passage. Jeremias points out that this saying cannot be understood as endorsing an abrogation of the Sabbath: "To take it as such is to lay all the accent on the first half of the saying, on the beatitude—Blessed is he who has understood the message of the Gospel, and who therefore knows that the time of Sabbath-keeping is over! But the stress can never fall on the first half of an antithetic parallelism. The abrupt vocative 'Man' indicates a stern rebuke, showing that Jesus, so far from intending to praise him, is taking him to task … So far from advocating the abrogation of the Sabbath, the intention of the logion is the exact opposite—to protect the Sabbath from frivolous neglect. If the story were an invention, it must have emanated from Jewish-Christian circles which stubbornly clung to the Sabbath (51)."

35 On the subject of non-canonical sayings of the Master, the *Gospel of Thomas* also transmits an otherwise unknown Sabbath-saying. According to *Thomas* 27, Yeshua told His disciples, "If you do not observe the Sabbath as a Sabbath, you will not see the Father."

36 Jerome, *On Matthew*, commentary on Matthew 12:13. See also, A.F.J. Klijn, *Jewish-Christian Gospel Tradition* (Supplements to Vigiliae Christianae 17; Leiden: E.J. Brill, 1993), 88.

37 Instone-Brewer, *Traditions of the Rabbis from the Era of the New Testament, Volume 2a: Feasts and Sabbaths: Passover and Atonement*, 43–45, 58–62.

38 Deuteronomy 17:8–13.

39 Matthew 23:2–3. Cf. Exodus 18:13–26.

40 "There is no strong tradition about him rejecting scribal ideas concerned with healing on the Sabbath. The defenses offered meet the requirements of scribal categories" (Basser, *Studies in Exegesis*, 19, 30).

41 Exodus 35:3.

42 b.*Shabbat* 133a.

43 b.*Shabbat* 147b–148a.

44 Lichtenstein, *Commentary on the New Testament*, on Matthew 12:8.

45 "Since the New Testament uses the expression 'lay hold of and lift,' we see the problem is one of rabbinical *muksteh*—'animals are not set

aside for Sabbath use'—and so must not be lifted." Basser, *Studies in Exegesis*, 21.

46. "No man shall assist a beast to give birth on the Sabbath day. And if it should fall into a cistern or pit, he shall not lift it out on the Sabbath." (CD 11:14); Geza Vermes, *The Dead Sea Scrolls in English* (New York, NY: Penguin Books, 1993), 110.

47. b.*Beitzah* 37a.

48. I.e., *a minori ad maius*.

49. The blessing is based upon Psalm 146:8: "The LORD opens the eyes of the blind. The LORD lifts up those who are bowed down."

50. Yechiel Tzvi Lichtenstein, *Commentary on the New Testament: The Holy Gospel According to Luke* (Unpublished, Marshfield, MO: Vine of David, 2010), on Luke 13:14; originally published in Hebrew: *Beiur LeSiphrei Brit HaChadashah* (Leipzig: Professor G. Dahlman, 1897). Sforno summarizes the ancient and medieval rabbinic tradition on this and similar Sabbath questions in his commentary on Exodus 31:15: "When it is possible to do a commandment on another day, the Sabbath is not moved aside for it." Basser, *Studies in Exegesis*, 23.

51. b.*Shabbat* 113a where the halachah permits the tying of and untying of such knots so long as they are not "permanent knots." The point of discussion is not identical to Luke 13, but rather it reflects a later development in Jewish law which apparently attempted to reconcile the necessity of tying and untying knots to care for livestock with the prohibition on knotting. The Mishnah discusses leading animals in and out on the Sabbath in m.*Shabbat* 5, and in m.*Eruvin* 2:1–2 the Mishnah provides instructions for making an *eruv* around a well to facilitate watering animals on the Sabbath. See *Torah Club Volume Four: Chronicles of the Messiah* commentary on Parashat Va'era for discussion on the Master's Sabbath conflicts and the meaning of Sabbath "work" (*melachah*).

52. David Instone-Brewer, *Traditions of the Rabbis from the Era of the New Testament*, vol. 2a: *Feasts and Sabbaths: Passover and Atonement*, 73.

53. It was probably the second meal, Saturday afternoon, after morning services in the Synagogue. Where did this happen? The anecdotes and teachings in Luke 14–17 are disconnected from any strict narrative or geographical progression. Although Luke has assembled them as a continuous narrative, they might have occurred at any time or place during the years of the Master's ministry.

54. b.*Eruvin* 63a.

55. b.*Bava Metzia* 59b. Cf. Deuteronomy 13:1–3.

56 See *Torah Club Volume Four: Chronicles of the Messiah* commentary on Parashat Va'era at Matthew 12:11–12. Some manuscripts of Luke 14:5 do not have a son falling into the well.

57 b.*Shabbat* 128b offers two opinions on the question. One allows helping the animal out of the pit, the second allows only bringing the animal fodder. The Qumran sect had stricter Sabbath laws than the Pharisees. According to the Dead Sea Scrolls (CD 11:13–17), "No one should help an animal give birth on the Sabbath; and if it falls into a well or a pit, he may not lift it out on the Sabbath ... Any living human who falls into a body of water or a cistern shall not be helped out with ladder, rope, or other instrument." *The Dead Sea Scrolls: A New Translation* (Michael Wise, Martin Abegg, Edward Cook, trans.; San Francisco: Harper San Francisco, 1996), 69.

58 Luke 13:15. See commentary on Luke 13:15 in *Torah Club Four: Chronicles of the Messiah*, Parashat Behar.

59 The laws prohibiting carrying on the Sabbath day are complex and involved, and they underwent significant development during the first century. It is difficult to know with much certainty exactly how they might have applied in John 5. The sages admit that "The laws of the Sabbath ... are like mountains hanging by a single hair, with few scriptures but many laws" (t.*Eruvin* 8:23). See Instone-Brewer, *Traditions of the Rabbis from the Era of the New Testament*, vol. 2a: *Feasts and Sabbaths—Passover and Atonement*, 23–36.

60 Numbers 15:32ff.

61 m.*Shabbat* 7:2.

62 Instone-Brewer, *Traditions of the Rabbis from the Era of the New Testament*, vol. 2a: *Feasts and Sabbaths—Passover and Atonement*, 42.

63 m.*Shabbat* 10:5.

64 John 5:13.

65 Yechiel Tzvi Lichtenstein, *Commentary on the New Testament: The Holy Gospel According to Yochanan* (Unpublished, Marshfield, MO: Vine of David, 2010), on John 5:17; originally published in Hebrew: *Beiur LeSiphrei Brit HaChadashah*, (Leipzig: Professor G. Dahlman, 1897).

66 *Genesis Rabbah* 11:6.

67 Cf. b.*Sanhedrin* 89b.

68 Today Judaism uses the term "*eruv*" to denote the boundary. The prescribed method of legally establishing shared ownership requires a communal loaf of bread in an established residence somewhere within the *eruv*. Some scholars see allusions to the practice of the shared meal and Sabbath *eruv* bread in 1 Corinthians 10:16–17: "The cup of blessing that we bless, is it not a participation in the

blood of Christ? The bread that we break, is it not a participation in the body of Christ? Because there is one bread, we who are many are one body, for we all partake of the one bread." One might also wonder if the statements in Acts that the believers held all things "in common" might not also be based, in part, upon the establishment of a common *eruv* (Acts 2:44; 4:32).

69   David Stern, *Jewish New Testament Commentary* (Clarksville, ML: Jewish New Testament Publications, Inc., 1999), 169.

70   Cf. b.*Shabbat* 81a–b; b.*Shabbat* 94b; b.*Menachot* 37b–38a.

71   t.*Eruvin* 3:8.

72   Cf. Matthew 24:16–18 where he warns his disciples to flee in haste, not returning home to pack their possessions before their flight. This implies that the question of baggage may be in view when he tells them to pray that their flight will not take place on the Sabbath.

73   John refers to Yeshua's challengers in this episode as "the Jews," which in this context should be read as Judean religious leaders. Are these Judean religious leaders from the party of the Pharisees or the Sadducees? Several clues point toward the Pharisees: 1) the Pharisees would be more concerned with halachic questions about the Sabbath than Sadducean leadership; 2) in John 5:25–29 Yeshua assumes that his challengers accept the belief in the resurrection of the dead; 3) in John 5:35 Yeshua assumes his challengers had high regard for John the Immerser; 4) in John 5:39, Yeshua assumes his challengers search the scriptures seeking eternal life. All of these point directly to the Pharisaic party. Papyrus Egerton 2, the oldest manuscript fragment containing text from John 5, refers to the Master's challengers as the "rulers of the people." If so, the Master engaged with some high-level sages among the Pharisees in John 5.

74   *Genesis Rabbah* 11:5.

75   "The expression [make oneself equal with God] in the Rabbinic sense implies some degree of 'rebellion' against the Divine government. A son who rejects the paternal authority is characterized as [one] who 'makes himself equal with his Father.' From the Rabbinic point of view the profanation of the Holy One which inhered in the words of J[esus] in vs. 17 consisted not in his calling the Holy One his Father, but in his presuming upon a peculiar sonship in virtue of which he had the right of performing the same 'continual work' as his Father. This was a blasphemy, equivalent to saying 'I am equal with,' as good as, 'my Father.'" Hugo Odeberg, *The Fourth Gospel* (Amsterdam, Holland: B.R. Guner, 1968), 203.

76   Fifth century CE *Athanasian Creed*, 32–34: "Perfect God and perfect man, of a reasonable soul and human flesh subsisting. Equal to the Father as touching his Godhead, and inferior to the Father as touching

his manhood. Who, although He is God and man, yet He is not two, but one Christ."

77 Raymond Brown, *The Gospel According to John I–XII* (vol. 29 of The Anchor Bible; New Haven: Yale University Press, 2006), 214.

78 The rabbis considered a father obligated to teach his son a trade: "A father is obligated to teach his son a trade … Rabbi Yehudah said, "One who does not teach his son a trade, teaches him to be a bandit" (b.*Kiddushin* 29a).

79 The Gospel of John does not preserve the Master's parables. Instead, John homogenizes them, along with the rest of Yeshua's teachings, into Johannine-style discourse. C.H. Dodd (*Historical Tradition in the Fourth Gospel* [Cambridge, 1963] 386, n. 2) says, "We have a perfectly realistic description of a son apprenticed to his father's trade. He does not act on his own initiative; he watched his father at work, and performs each operation as his father performs it. The affectionate father shows the boy all the secrets of his craft. So far there is no single expression which is not appropriate in describing a situation in real life. The passage is a true parable … applied in allegorical fashion, in a classical exposition of basic Johannine Christology."

80 E.g., b.*Sotah* 14a: "Just as the Holy One, blessed be He, clothes the naked, as it is written [in Genesis 3:21], 'The LORD God made garments of skin for Adam and his wife, and clothed them,' so too should you also clothe the naked. The Holy One, blessed be He, visited the sick, as it is written [in Genesis 18:1], 'Now the LORD appeared to him by the oaks of Mamre,' [while he was still recovering from circumcision,] so too should you also visit the sick. The Holy One, blessed be He, comforted mourners, as it is written [in Genesis 25:11], 'After the death of Abraham, that God blessed his son Isaac,' so too should you also comfort mourners. The Holy one, blessed be He, buried the dead, as it is written [in Deuteronomy 34:6], 'And He buried him in the valley in the land of Moab,' so too should you also bury the dead."

81 John 5. According to the Johannine narrative, that incident must have occurred at least twelve months earlier. When the story is harmonized with the Synoptic Gospels, the incident could have happened more than two years earlier.

82 John 5:17–47. See *Torah Club Volume Four: Chronicles of the Messiah* on Parashat Vayigash.

83 I.e., *a minori ad maius*, a common method of rabbinic argumentation.

84 The Mishnah describes how the Sabbath can be broken in order to deliver a baby. This falls into the category of *pikkuach nefesh*, breaking the Sabbath to save a life. Then the Mishnah derives the permission to circumcise on Shabbat. The argument runs thus: If it is permissible

to break the Sabbath to deliver a child, it must be permissible to break the Sabbath to circumcise that same child eight days later. "They deliver a woman's baby on the Sabbath [even if it requires violating the Sabbath]. They will summon a midwife from a distant place, and they violate the Sabbath on account of the mother. They [also violate the Sabbath when they] tie the umbilical cord. Rabbi Yosi said, 'They also cut it.' Likewise, they perform everything necessary for a circumcision on the Sabbath" (m.*Shabbat* 18:3). The Mishnah provides a vivid description of how many ways the Sabbath must be broken in order to carry out the circumcision: "They perform everything necessary for a circumcision on the Sabbath. They cut, tear, suction, dress with poultice and cumin …" (m.*Shabbat* 19:2).

85 m.*Nedarim* 3:11.

86 Rabbi Akiva made a similar argument based upon the Temple service: "Did the Torah impose greater stringency on the Temple service or on the Sabbath? It was more stringent in regard to the Temple service than the Sabbath, for the Temple service overrides the prohibitions of the Sabbath, but the Sabbath does not override the Temple service. Now argue the matter from the light to heavy (*kal vachomer*). If the Temple service supersedes the prohibitions of the Sabbath and a matter of potentially saving a life overrides it [i.e., the Temple service], how much more so should the potential of saving a life supersede the Sabbath, which is superseded by the Temple service. Thus you have learned that the potential of saving a life overrides the Sabbath" (t.*Shabbat* 15:17).

87 C.K. Barrett, *The Gospel According to St. John: An Introduction with Commentary and Notes on the Greek Text* (2d ed.; Philadelphia, PA: The Westminster Press, 1978), 320.

88 Yechiel Tzvi Lichtenstein, *Commentary on the New Testament: The Holy Gospel According to Yochanan* (Unpublished, Marshfield, MO: Vine of David, 2010), on Mark 3:4; originally published in Hebrew: *Beiur LeSiphrei Brit HaChadashah* (Leipzig: Professor G. Dahlman, 1897), on John 7:22.

89 m.*Avot* 1:2.

90 m.*Shabbat* 7:2.

91 E.g., "A man once came before Rabbi Chaninah and testified to him, 'I am sure that this man is the firstborn.' Chaninah asked, 'How is it that you are certain of this?' The man said, 'Because when [sick] people came to his father he would tell them, "Go to my son Shikhath. He is firstborn and his spittle heals."' Might he not have been the firstborn of his mother [and not of his father]? [No, because] there is a tradition that the spittle of the firstborn of a father heals, but that of the firstborn of a mother does not heal" (b.*Bava Batra* 126b).

92 y.*Avodah Zarah* 14d cited in George Beasley-Murray, *John* (vol. 36, 2 ed., of Word Biblical Commentary; Nashville, TN: Thomas Nelson, 1999), 157.

93 Matthew 12:5.

94 Numbers 15:32–36; Exodus 16:29.

95 See tractate *Shabbat*.

96 Aryeh Kaplin, *The Sabbath: Day of Eternity*, The Aryeh Kaplan Anthology (vol. 2; Brooklyn, NY: Mesorah Publications, Ltd., 1995), 140.

97 Nehemiah 13:15–18.

98 b.*Shabbat* 113a where the halachah permits the tying of and untying of such knots so long as they are not "permanent knots." The point of discussion is not identical to Luke 13, but rather it reflects a later development in Jewish law, which apparently attempted to reconcile the necessity of tying and untying knots to care for livestock with the prohibition on knotting. The Mishnah discusses leading animals in and out on the Sabbath in m.*Shabbat* 5, and in m.*Eruvin* 2:1–2 the Mishnah provides instructions for making an *eruv* around a well to facilitate watering animals on the Sabbath.

99 Matthew 12:5.

100 The uncertainty in the area of electricity and Shabbat has mostly to do with the fact that the technology of electricity developed at such a late time. There are no authoritative courts or precedents or early commentators on which to base the decision.

101 Amos 8:5; Nehemiah 10:31–32, 13:15–21.

102 1 Corinthians 16:2.

103 Nehemiah 13:15–18.

104 b.*Shabbat* 75b.

105 m.*Avot* 1:2.

www.ingramcontent.com/pod-product-compliance
Lightning Source LLC
Chambersburg PA
CBHW071209070526
44584CB00019B/2973